Langone

Like, love, lust.

DATE DUE

JUL 1 6 1984		
JUL 2 3 1985		
APR 1 0 1986		
MAR 1 4 1987		
MAR 3 0 1987		
FEB - 3 1989		
APR 1 2 1990		
DEC 3 1990		
201-6503		Printed in USA

Other Books by John Langone

DEATH IS A NOUN
A View of the End of Life

GOODBYE TO BEDLAM
Understanding Mental Illness and Retardation

BOMBED, BUZZED, SMASHED, OR . . . SOBER
A Book about Alcohol

HUMAN ENGINEERING
Marvel or Menace?

Like, Love, Lust

Like, Love, Lust

A VIEW OF SEX AND SEXUALITY

by John Langone

Little, Brown and Company
BOSTON   TORONTO

FIRST EDITION

Library of Congress Cataloging in Publication Data

Langone, John 1929–
  Like, Love, Lust.

   Bibliography: p.
   Includes index.
   SUMMARY: Discusses the ethics of sex and love, including the related topics of homosexuality, jealousy, pornography, prostitution, marriage, and living together.
   1. Sexual ethics — Juvenile literature.   2. Love — Juvenile literature.   3. Interpersonal relations — Juvenile literature.   [1. Sexual ethics.   2. Love. 3. Interpersonal relations]   I. Title.
HQ31.L256   301.41   79-26428
ISBN 0-316-51429-2

BP

*Published simultaneously in Canada
by Little, Brown & Company (Canada) Limited*

PRINTED IN THE UNITED STATES OF AMERICA

For my sister, Mary Theresa

Acknowledgments

THIS BOOK WAS COMPLETED while the writer was a Fellow at the Center for Advanced Study in the Behavioral Sciences at Stanford, California. I am grateful for financial support provided by the National Science Foundation — grant no. BNS 76–22943 A02.

Wherever possible, sources used have been cited either within the text or in the back notes. Journals, news releases from universities and medical centers, and material from government agencies, all of which were made available through my membership in the National Association of Science Writers, were most valuable.

My special thanks to my dear friend Paula McArdle, a student at Emmanuel College in Boston, who helped gather the young people's comments that appear herein.

Palo Alto, California
February 1979

Contents

Like, Love, Lust

Introduction

The advertisement — you may have seen it — depicts an exquisitely wrought bracelet bearing seven silver charms, each a beautiful, sculptured flower, each conveying a secret message. The language of these flowers, the ad tells us, goes like this:

"You are beautiful," murmurs the daisy.
"The light of my life," adds the twining honeysuckle.
"I love you," chants the amorous rose.
"My love is constant," declares the delicate veronica.
"And steadfast," whispers the modest violet.
"Accept my devotion," pleads the heliotrope.
And the little forget-me-not repeats its name, "Forget me not . . . forget me not."

Love — need I say it? — is what it's all about. Love. The solid sterling, glittering gold and sparkling diamond of our emotions, the universal human experience that elevates the spirit, quickens the pulse, makes Silly Putty of the brain and parting such sweet sorrow. It is the warm, positive feeling we have for another, a feeling that includes a desire to remain close to, to touch, that person. It can also make us sick and jealous and even suicidal, and it has been known to turn into its opposite, hate, or coexist with it.

Wrought in the soul and wrung from the heart, love is the stuff of poem and song, of valentine and philosophy, and virtually every culture, modern and primitive, has had something to say about it. Our most sought-after and cherished ideal, it is, as the balladeers have written and sung, what makes the world go 'round, a many-splendored thing whose magic spell is everywhere. "All you need is love," sing the Beatles. "I love you, I honestly love you," sighs Olivia Newton-John. It is there, also, when the young Spaniard plays his guitar in the custom known as *las mañanitas*, waking his beloved on her birthday with a joyful dawn serenade. It is there, this lyric expression of devotion, changed somewhat, in the American black's melancholy blues, in the tragic and fateful fado songs of Portugal, in the haunting, sad folk song of the Sephardic Jews that tells of the shepherdess who rejects an adoring boy "because he is too young for love." It is the English romantic poet Samuel Taylor Coleridge intoning, "All thoughts, all passions, all delights, / Whatever stirs this mortal frame, / All are but ministers of Love, / And feed his sacred flame." It is the Old Testament's Jacob seeking Rachel's hand in marriage, forced to serve her father for seven years, then seven more for the privilege, "and they seemed but a few days, because of the greatness of his love." It is a youthful Romeo in the famous balcony scene with Juliet, delivering immortal lines: "But, soft! what light through yonder window breaks? It is the east, and Juliet is the sun!" Love it was that sent Orpheus, the musician of Greek mythology, into Hades to find his wife, Eurydice; Lancelot to the rescue of Queen Guinevere; Isolde to her death with Tristan in the Wagnerian opera of love eternal.

And we read of places where nightingales their lovesick ditties sing, and of love knots tied as a symbol of loyalty, of heartfelt *billets-doux,* or love letters.

"If I had wings," Benjamin Franklin wrote to Mme. Brillon, "I think I should have flown to you, and I think I should sometimes scratch on the window of your bedchamber. It is very mischievous of nature to deny us the advantages that she wastes so profusely on all the little good-for-nothing birds and flies." Napoleon Bonaparte put it another way in a note to the Polish Countess Walewska: "I saw none but you. I admired none but you. Answer at once, and still the impatient ardor of N."

We have love taps and loving cups, lovebirds and love potions. Take the juice of the flower *Viola tricolor,* known also as love-in-idleness, and apply it to sleeping eyes, and it will cause love for the first living object seen after awakening. Or so the story goes. A Creole recipe, guaranteed to bring about love, calls for a roasted hummingbird heart ground into powder and sprinkled on the object of affection.

Love dances to show off beauty and to prove the endurance of deep affection are common to many cultures, and love chases, from Li'l Abner's Sadie Hawkins Day to the ancient Greeks' Pelops-Hippodameia contests, offer the prize of a mate. Among the Mongolians, a maiden was placed on a horse and given a whip and the right to use it on both animal and the men who chased her. She was given to the man who caught her.

And when we are forsaken by love, we are forlorn and pining, lovelorn, country-western broken hearted. And there is a flower named after this feeling—the red amaranth, called love-lies-bleeding, whose root is so weak that it falls and lies prostrate in the garden.

In contrast to directing our love toward one special person, there is also love for a group, for brotherhood and sisterhood. There were the hippie love-ins of the sixties, all incense and beads, psychedelic fashion shows of flowered pants and colorful robes, and hearts painted on foreheads, with lapel buttons proclaiming, "Love." Flowers over the ears, youth went barefoot and dancing a daisy chain to the chant of, "Love us, join us, peace and love, turn on, tune in, make love not war." Their theme, love thy neighbor, was an old one, not very much different from that of agape, love feasts celebrated by early Christians in token of brotherly love. Its public demonstration drew this comment from the Reverend Kenneth B. Murphy, a Boston priest and social activist:

> Perhaps they do dress weird, but what is the most important feature, the heart or the style? In a world that is trying to tear itself to shreds and where protests of all kinds have become the order of the day, it is refreshing to see that love and concern for one's fellow man can hold sway. . . . If love comes with long hair and a beard and clothes that seem outlandish to the majority of the community, is it any the less sincere? When they say "love" they are practicing what we preach. When four thousand youngsters gather for no purpose other than to be together in a harmony of mind and spirit, there is a teaching there for us all.[1]

Music, too, the priest said, is the best explanation young people have for themselves. "Much of what is written and played is incomprehensible to most adults. Too much of it deals with drugs or the false crutch of intellectualizing this social ill. But so much more of it is good common-sense dealing with human relationships."

All of this, as you can see, has to do with feelings directed toward individuals, singly or in groups. In its purest form, however, love may be regarded by some as God's greatest gift, the very essence of divinity, a tendency of the soul toward good. "When you love, you should not say, 'God is in my heart,' " wrote poet Kahlil Gibran in *The Prophet,* "but rather, 'I am in the heart of God.' " We love, say the theologians, because every person's soul is created by God in His own image and likeness, and this makes us one spiritually. We love so that we can become one with God. Plato believed that while love burst upon us all, primed by the sight of a beautiful body, the final goal is a supreme beauty from which all other beauties come, an eternal good to which we aspire. Admiring and desiring someone beautiful, then, might be seen as a step toward the absolute beauty, just as the scholar's studies aim him or her toward ultimate wisdom. Saint Augustine, the church father and moral theologian, has also given us a detailed analysis of love. In his youth, he was a petty thief who enjoyed stealing for its own sake, and he had numerous sexual escapades that brought him much selfish pleasure. The death of a close friend brought him to his senses, he wrote, and the result was his complete love of God and knowledge of the Divine.

But while there are those who would argue, and probably rightfully, that true love can exist only between rational beings and may be directed only toward God or toward a neighbor who can return the affection, it is also there, or at least we think it is, every time, as someone said, we pat a cat, wax a car, eat a steak, name a boat, kiss a gun. "Don't you just *love* the way Carly Simon sings?" you might gush to a friend. Or, "I *love* double-chocolate but hate pistachio."

There is no question that the word is misused and misunderstood, and in applying it to so many things, as we do, we are not only imprecise, but are diluting its worth, its power to blot out fear and hatred and to transform the world. It is no wonder, amid all the inappropriate uses of the word, that so often *love* is a synonym for *lust,* for having sex, a four-letter word that changes the meaning of *making love* to "making out."

In the pages ahead, we'll be talking about love, what it is and what it is not. We'll examine the scientific aspects of love, the new insights into its meaning that psychologists are presenting today, and how these differ from what was believed when love was first put under the microscope in the late 1800s. We'll talk about sex, because sexual intimacy has a definite and important place in our lives, and about its relationship to love. But this is not a book about the art and technique of lovemaking, about the physical aspects of sex. Presuming that you all have taken sex education courses, that you already know something about sex, this book will emphasize some of the things that you sometimes don't hear too much about in sex education classes, things like showing tenderness, caring, sharing, communication. We'll look at liking and friendship, love's close relatives, and at living together and marriage and jealousy. And we'll talk about some other topics not generally treated in books for this age group — prostitution, pornography, homosexuality and the philosophy behind sex education, along with the controversy over teaching or not teaching it to you.

In summary, this book won't tell you how to solve personal "affairs of the heart," whether you should take birth control pills, put an illegitimate baby up for adoption, or have an abortion. It is not a collection of letters and responses culled from newspaper or magazine columns of advice for teenagers. But it will, I hope, help you to relate better to others and understand what loving and liking and friendship are all about, what the difference is between indiscriminate sex and sex in a relationship that is meaningful, and what it means to say that really loving someone is wanting what is best for him or her, not what is best for ourselves.

1

Friendship/Liking/Loving

We have all heard that a friend in need is a friend indeed; that love is displayed by laying down one's life for one's friends; and that faithful are the wounds of a friend, but the kisses of an enemy are deceitful. Or as Cicero, the great Roman orator, put it, "Every man can tell how many goats or sheep he possesses, but not how many friends."

Friendship. It has been praised as a state of mutual affection, one of life's nobler possessions, a gift that enables us to ignore the flaws and foibles of those we favor. Appreciated more if it is lost, friendship keeps us honest, makes us confident, lifts our moods.

Much has been written about friendship as a congenial union that operates irrespective of sex, color and creed. And love cannot be discussed, as it will be in this chapter, without first referring to friendship and to the inclination that touches it off: liking.

In Charlotte Brontë's novel *Shirley,* there is this bit of dialogue:

"Be responsible, Louis — be patient! I like you because you are patient."

"Like me no longer, then — love me instead."

Each of us, no doubt, has wondered about the difference between liking and loving, or we've asked whether they are actually the same. Sometimes we're not sure whether we like or love someone. Other times, when we're questioned about how we feel, we're more certain — or at least we give that impression. "Just a friend," we say assuredly. Or, "A very close friend, no more than that." Or even, "I just love him/her, that's all, it's that simple." Comfortable though we may be with such responses, they are not really answers at all. Actor Lee Marvin, during a recent, highly publicized suit brought against him by a woman with whom he lived for some time, touched upon the difficulty of defining a feeling of affection. In a letter, Marvin referred to his friend as "my love." The rest of the courtroom dialogue went like this:

"Was she your love?"

"No," said Marvin. "That's an English figure of speech."

"Did you want her to love you?"

"I don't think so."

"Did she tell you she loved you?"

"On occasion."

"Did you tell her you loved her?"

"On occasion."

"But you didn't really mean it, did you?"

"No."

Later, Marvin compared being in love to the fuel gauge on a car, saying that his love for the woman had never got beyond "half a tank." At one point, he added, it had been "one-quarter full, a girlfriend-boyfriend feeling."

As the material for this book was gathered, a number of high school students were asked how they viewed liking and loving. Some of their replies are typical of the problems we all have with the answer. "Liking is when you like a friend," said one junior high school girl. "But it's not love. That's almost married." Another student said, "Liking is when you like each other and pal around together. Loving is when you do other stuff." Observed another, "Liking is not having the same feeling when you're away from a friend for a long time as you have when you're away from your lover." Said another, "When you like someone, you just hang around them for a while. When you love them, you act strange, you make out." In utter frustration, a sixteen-year-old put it this way: "Loving is not the same as liking because liking is when you like someone and loving is when you love someone."

One point should be clearly made. Just as the lines that separate the various categories of human behavior, political theory, religion and science are not always boldly drawn, so, too, is there some hesitation when it comes down to a firm definition of *like* and *love*. Our thoughts and feelings are much too intricate to be put into neat compartments, and there are all sorts of blends, shades of gray, in this world that is peopled with so many different individuals. An intensely close relationship may develop between a man and a woman. They enjoy each other's company regularly. They exchange confidences, they show concern for one another, they ignore one another's faults, they miss each other when apart. Are they simply close friends, or are they lovers? Suppose that these two have not been sexually intimate, that passion has never played a part in the relationship.

Does this mean that they do not love each other? On the other hand, what if this couple does have sex? Are they "in love"?

It is often said that we can like people a whole lot and not love them. Or even that we can love someone — a mother or father or brother, for instance — and still not like them very much because, maybe, they bore or embarrass us. There are, of course, no absolute answers to the questions asked above. It is not easy to firmly define *like* and *love*. Each situation must be examined carefully and thoughtfully, each individual and circumstance considered. Liking, loving and friendship are intertwined, sometimes closely, sometimes loosely. Each involves a certain feeling between people, a warmth, an affection, a mixing of minds.

Against that background of caution, it can be said that while there is a common denominator in liking and loving, there are some significant differences between the two. Some students came close to the mark. "Love is deep, liking is superficial," said one. "Loving is special, liking is not," said another. "You cannot love unless you have given part of yourself, put yourself second." Or as someone else put it, somewhat facetiously, "Love is when your boyfriend holds you in his arms and comforts you after you just smashed up his car."

Implicit in what these students have said is that liking and loving differ in strength and warmth, and in the depth of involvement.

Defining love metaphorically, as the young people and the poets and songwriters have done, is not very scientific (although perhaps describing what it feels like to be in love in nonscientific terms is sometimes as valuable, maybe more so, as trying to dissect it as you would a laboratory frog). So, with the hope that too close a look at love won't ruin the nice feeling it brings, consider, for a bit, what science has to say about love. But before beginning, be aware that not everyone agrees it's worth examining scientifically.

A few years ago, Senator William Proxmire of Wisconsin issued a statement saying that his choice at that time for the biggest waste of the taxpayers' money was the thousands of dollars spent by the National Science Foundation to determine why people fall in love. The senator called it a "futile and wasteful attempt to define the impossible," and said that no one, not even the National Science Foundation, could argue that falling in love is a science. The scientists involved replied that their work was essential because close relationships are directly related to issues like marriage and divorce, which are vital social considerations.

While it is true, as Senator Proxmire has said, that a precise definition of love is not possible, behavioral scientists have been studying the subject for many years, and they do know a great deal about it. Bearing in mind that there are differences of opinion in the broad field of human behavior, it can be said with some degree of certainty that love is not a biological drive, like sex, that demands to be satisfied.

"It certainly is not a biological need," says psychologist Theodore Reik, "because there are millions of people who do not feel it and many centuries and cultural patterns in which it is unknown. We cannot name any inner secretions or specific glands which are responsible for it. Sex is originally objectless. Love certainly is not. It is a very definite, emotional relationship between a Me and a You." Sex, Reik points out, is common to both men and beasts, but love is the result of cultural development. "Sex can be casual about its object, love cannot. Love is always a personal relationship. This is not necessarily so with sex. . . . There is need of variety in sex, but not in love. The sex object can be easily replaced, but not the love-object. There are many possible sexual objects, but only one who is loved."[1]

Reik is quite right. Sex and love are very different. Sex is physiological and biochemical, love is emotional. As the psychologist puts it, "Sex is an urge, love is a desire."

But for centuries, human beings have confused the two. Men have searched, and continue to search, for ways to stimulate the sex drive, and thus enhance love, and whenever they think they have found a chemical way to achieve that, it becomes popularly known as a love potion, or an aphrodisiac, named after Aphrodite, the Greek goddess of love. It is true that some modern experimental drugs can be powerful *sex* stimulants. We can also inject a person with the hormone adrenaline, and he or she will experience the same reactions that we associate with love — heart palpitations, flushing and heavy breathing. But these substances and responses have little to do with love. No pill, no drink of liquor, no puff on a joint, no dab of perfume can make us love. Sex is, of course, an essential part of love between a man and a woman, but it is not the heart of it. Love, as we will see next, develops from childhood, and thus it is there long before we are attracted sexually by someone. Moreover, as Reik tells us, it can outlive and outwear sex.

Early psychologists, who didn't give love as much attention as it gets today, believed that it was instinctive behavior, that is, something that occurred naturally without any prompting. Sigmund Freud, the founder of psychoanalysis, taught that instinctive, biological drives that need to be gratified are what power our behavior from childhood. Love, he felt, was based in the sex drive, or the libido. He defined the latter as "the energy of those instincts which have to do with all that may be comprised under the word, love." According to Freud, we all pass through a series of psychosexual stages, in which pleasure-seeking plays an important part. In psychology, in fact, the most common definition of love one encounters relates to pleasure, generally as it applies to satisfying experiences between members of opposite sexes. And there is no question that we seek pleasure. The newborn baby first seeks only to gratify itself, and it loves, if we may even use the word, only itself. Later, it loves the mother because she is the one who feeds and comforts, and it is made aware at the same time that the mother returns that love. The mother's facial expressions, gestures and comforting sounds are clues to the love for the child, and the child, even at an early age, senses them.

Today, we can say with reasonable certainty that love is learned behavior, something we develop by our associations with others and by our own acquired attitudes. Love is a feeling, a strong one that is influenced by our environment and our culture. Sex comes along, of course, with our biological inheritance, and it undoubtedly plays a role in whom we love and how. But layered over that instinctive drive, over that seeking after pleasure, are the things that we learn later, the things that enable us to modify, to improve, that instinctive behavior so that it becomes more than sexual attraction, more than merely liking. We learn, for instance, to extend our early love for our parents to others, and we learn how to alter it to fit individuals. But sometimes we don't learn. Psychologists have shown that children who have been raised in an unfavorable environment — that is, one of parental absence, and absence of other, substitute, parent figures — or who have uncaring or harsh parents, may well grow up ignorant of what love is. As adults, they may be unable to form lasting friendships and other relationships. If, for example, their parents have been overly critical and domineering, the children might suffer from low self-esteem. They might always feel that they are not good enough for anyone, and might have a difficult time showing love, often out of fear of being rejected. If love were instinctive, such would not be the case. The person's genetic code would, in effect, spell out *love,* and this would enable him or her to overcome, automatically, all obstacles in the way of loving. This doesn't happen.

Some psychologists have carried the idea even further. One recent university study of three hundred women in Syracuse, New York, suggests that women who rarely experience orgasm (the climax of sexual excitement) had fathers who were distant, absent, or casual and permissive in raising their daughters. The study indicated also that the women who got more pleasure out of sex were more likely to have been brought up by fathers who were caring and who insisted that the girls live up to certain moral standards.

Raising this issue does not contradict our earlier statements that sex is not love. For although it is not that, a satisfying sexual relationship is often important to the course of love, particularly if we know how to make our partners happy as well as ourselves. We cannot discount the fact that men and women are attracted to one another sexually; use the word *physically,* if you prefer. Sometimes we're not aware the attraction is there, other times we won't admit to it. The normal biological conclusion of that attraction is intercourse. But, again, we learn how to modify our instinctive drives, to control them. And most of the time, we are successful.

But to return to the discussion about the importance of parental affection in the growth process that teaches us to love, Professor Philip G. Zimbardo, who teaches psychology at Stanford University, tells an interesting story that emphasizes how essential love and affection are to infants. The story involves Frederick II, a thirteenth-century Sicilian ruler and a master of languages, who believed that every person was born with the knowledge of some ancient language. According to Frederick, this language would show itself, without any training or experience, as soon as the child was old enough. Learning would be necessary only to perfect the innate language. To test this theory, Frederick put a group of foster mothers in charge of newborn infants. They were instructed to care for the babies, but were never to speak to them or to allow them to hear human sounds. Frederick believed that when they did finally speak, they would reveal only their buried, inherited language; being brought up in silence would ensure that, since they would not be influenced by any other. Professor Zimbardo quotes the unexpected result of this drastic experiment: "But he labored in vain, because the children all died. For they could not live without the petting and the joyful faces and loving words of their foster mothers."[2]

One would not, of course, perform such an experiment on humans today. But something like it has been done with monkeys, and the results show that not only human beings, but animals too, are affected by a lack of close contact with a caring parent. Proof of this has come from the classic studies of psychologist Harry F. Harlow, now at the University of Wisconsin. Dr. Harlow, who studied primate behavior for some forty years, separated baby monkeys from their mothers and found that the babies subsequently would huddle in the corners of their cages, crying and refusing to associate with other monkeys.

Harlow's studies have also shown that infant female monkeys who have been raised without natural mothers do not become good mothers themselves. These "motherless mothers" become cruel and either ignore their offspring or physically abuse them, sometimes violently. Today we know that parents who harm their children — in what is known as the "battered child syndrome" — often act abusively because as children they themselves were deprived of love, or were beaten.

Love, then, is something we learn how to show and feel if we have been exposed to it and given it. I love, you love, he and she love, we all love — not because we are born with it in our genes but because we have slowly acquired the capacity for it. It is a word of only four letters, *love,* but it contains a host of other words. Psychologists call all of the ingredients that make up love "dimensions" or "components." Margaret N. Reedy of the Andrus Gerontology Center at the University of Southern California (whose study on the age differences in satisfying love relationships will be discussed in the chapter on marriage) has compiled a valuable list of these components. There are six of them. First, there is emotional security, referring to feelings of trust, caring, concern and warmth. Next comes respect, which means the ability to be tolerant, understanding and patient. Third is the fact that lovers enjoy being able to spend time together working as well as playing. Fourth is communication, the ability to be honest and self-revealing, and a good listener, too. The fifth component of love is loyalty, or a sense of investment and commitment to the future of the relationship. The sixth is sexual intimacy, which, as we know, involves sexual attraction, passionate desire and pleasurable lovemaking.

Again, these components are not coded in our genes, no more than are their opposites — mistrust, disrespect, intolerance, dishonesty, infidelity, coldness. Every one of them, the desirable ones and the undesirable, can be learned. And the amount of love you are able to show, as well as the amount you are able to give, will depend on how many of these components you possess.

Sometimes, when we can't learn at home, we can learn from friends. They can show us the wrong way and the right way, depending on how they've learned and from whom. They can show us the way through those dimensions of love, or they can block it. Which brings us back to liking and friendship, those two close allies of love, whose help we need if we are to love.

Recall that liking was defined as a feeling of affection. When we enjoy someone's company, we like that person. Sex does not have to play a part in it, because liking and the friendship that grows from it are peak experiences in themselves. Another feature of liking is that it can be directed at many individuals; that is, we can like many different people, have many different friends and acquaintances, and for different reasons. Mike shares your interest in literature, but not your interest in music. That doesn't mar your friendship with Mike, however, and you are able to discuss music with your friend Mary. She, in turn, enjoys sailing, which you do not, and she has friends who share that interest. This variety in friends, this ability to like one person for one quality and someone else for another, is good for us. For one thing, it enables us to display parts of our many-sided personalities. For another, it keeps an edge on mutual interests; liking a specific someone allows us to learn more about those things, and our education is thus broadened.

Being able to like someone is valuable, even if the affection you feel is but a flicker. You like the way a person dresses or wears his hair or swims, and it pleases you to watch him. You enjoy someone's behavior at a party, and you look forward to having her around on certain occasions. In cases like these, liking brings us pleasure, and may even prod us into improving ourselves. The more friends and acquaintances we have, then, the fuller our lives will be, the more opportunity we will have to learn how best to practice those six dimensions that spell out love.

The problem with many of us, however, is that we tend to seek out one "good friend," one confidant who understands us as perfectly as we understand him or her. In situations like that, jealousy eventually intrudes, and the friendship, based as it is on selfishness, usually dissolves. It is important to understand that when we look for the one perfect friend, we are not only chasing a mirage, but we are limiting our options. That is, we are cutting ourselves off from others who can help us enrich our lives, even in small ways. Two "perfect" friends who dote on one another and exclude others from their Siamese-twin act generally end up boring each other — not to mention those who know them — because of their limited view of the world.

Friendships are important, but what about the reasons behind our choice of friends? Why do we like certain individuals and dislike, even abhor, others? How do we choose our friends? Do we pick them because they'll listen to our problems? Because they share our interests?

Again, just as it is not easy to define *like* and *love,* there is no one way to explain why we make the choices we do when seeking our friends. Each of us has his or her own reasons, and these may or may not differ from friend to friend. Most psychologists believe, however, that we usually like the most those who praise us, who are competent in their jobs and successful in their private lives, and who generally agree with our views. A few years ago, at a unique symposium at Connecticut College on love, attraction, passion and power, several speakers remarked that one can predict quite well how much a person will like another if it is known to what extent the other rewards or punishes. If, for example, you find out that someone you are to be introduced to has expressed a good deal of interest in your work, has spoken favorably of your talent or is known to be less than critical as a general rule, you might look forward to meeting that person, maybe thinking, "You and I are going to get along really well." Also, if you learn that someone is in the habit of doing favors, or giving gifts, you might be influenced by that. And if you're the sort of person who values such things, it should be fairly easy to predict who you will and will not like. On the other hand, it is not unusual for individuals to experience intense liking or love for people who have rejected them. In line with that, there is the example of the woman who discovers her husband is seeing someone else. The pain and suffering the wife experiences at this discovery may cause her to realize how much she loves her husband. And there are the lovers who pine for women who ignore them, like the Italian lover of a few years back who kidnapped his former sweetheart, saying, "The fact that she rejected me only made me want and love her more." Harvard sociologist George C. Homans, who was also at the Connecticut College meeting, observed, "I believe that a man is apt to be strongly attracted to another person who punishes him fairly, provided that the punishment enables him to learn to perform actions that ultimately win him highly valued rewards. Just as some of us learn to bite the hand that feeds us, others learn to lick the hand that beats us."

Other people choose friends from those who have a strong need to be cared for, people who have not matured enough to stand on their own, even people who are too ill, physically, to tend to their own needs. It is not always wrong to select friends of that sort because such individuals, of course, need friends, too. But there are people who always seek and hold on to such dependent friends — as well as those who accept more than the usual amount of tender, loving care — and in doing so they may have warped the meaning of friendship. They may be using the relationship for selfish ends — that is, they desperately need being leaned on to survive. It is a dangerous emotional trap, both for the person who is dependent, and for the person who consistently offers a shoulder to cry on.

In his ethical treatise, the *Nicomachean Ethics,* the great philosopher Aristotle discussed this idea of selfishness. "To be friends, men must (1) feel good-will for each other, that is, wish each other's good; (2) be aware of each other's good-will; (3) the cause of their good-will must be one of the three lovable qualities, i.e., the goodness, or pleasantness, or usefulness of their friend." The philosopher takes issue with so-called friends whose affection is based on utility — for example, the candidate for election who is "friendly" to voters, or the salesman who joins a social club to meet potential customers — or purely on pleasure. "In a friendship based on utility or pleasure," says Aristotle,

men love their friends for their own good or their own pleasure: they love him not for what he is, but for being useful or agreeable. And, therefore, these friendships are based on an accident since the friend is not loved for being what he is, but as affording some benefit or pleasure as the case may be. Consequently, friendships of this kind are easily broken off, in the event of the parties themselves changing, for if no longer pleasant or useful to each other, they cease to love each other. And utility is not a permanent quality; it differs at different times. Hence, when the motive of the friendship has passed away, the friendship is dissolved, having existed merely as a means to that end.[3]

Physical attractiveness is another reason we seek out others. It may not be the best reason, but it is, nonetheless, a factor. "Generally speaking," says Stanford's Professor Zimbardo, "we like beautiful people more than we like homely ones. . . . One reason is that we have a stereotyped notion that whatever is beautiful is good. Thus we perceive beautiful people as more intelligent, more successful, more pleasant, and happier than other people, even if there is no objective basis for these judgments." Thus far, he points out, research on physical attractiveness has been conducted among people who did not know each other or who were beginning to get acquainted. "It may be," says Zimbardo, "that physical attractiveness plays a more important role in these initial 'getting to know you' stages than later on in a relationship."[4]

There are lessons here for us all, young and old. It's not a bad idea to take a closer look, every so often, at our friends, the ones we've had as well as the ones we have now. Ask yourself questions about their likes and dislikes, about their manners, their habits, appearance and abilities. Ask yourself why you like each one. Are they mirror images of you now or as you used to be? Or do they have ideal qualities that you do not have but wish you did? On the other hand, do you think you'd like your friend more if he or she made a mistake every so often, did something really stupid? Ask yourself whether you like your friends because you can push them around, because they won't make a move without you. Or do you like someone because you can't make a move without him? What about your other relationships, those with your teachers, for instance? Do you favor your math teacher because he's easy on you, because he really knows his subject, because he takes time to help, or because he's cute? Do you like the boss on your part-time job because he or she doesn't bug you if you come in late?

It's a good idea, too, to think a little more about the nature of friendship itself, about its importance in our lives. Robert Brain, the noted anthropologist-sociologist, feels that friendship must be taken as seriously as sex, aggression and marriage. We have become estranged, he says, from the simple human tendency to cling together, which is taken for granted in other cultures, and for too long have turned a blind eye to friendship needs, to the pain of loneliness and separation and the psychological damage it can cause. "Psychologists have found that friends are needed to concretize a man's world, to discover his complete human personality," he says. "That is why the dialogue of the confessional or the psychotherapist's couch sometimes provide the only outlets for friendless and lonely people. . . . I have no qualms in elevating friendship into an imperative."[5]

Examining the concept of friendship, as well as the friends and others in your life, will ultimately tell you a great deal about yourself, and help you build a better self-image — if you're honest about the answers. Liking yourself is the goal, an essential, as will be seen, in loving and being loved.

2

Knowing, and Liking, Yourself

ONE OF THE MOST IMPORTANT FACTS you should know about yourself is that you are not, as an old song told us, "nothing but a nothing, not a thing at all." Rather, each and every one of you is a totally unique individual, a very special person whose parts have been organized with great care. True, we're all made up of the same chemicals, the same flesh and bone and tissue. The arrangement, however, is different for each of us, as individual as our fingerprints.

Sometimes all the parts don't work smoothly, particularly the ones involving our emotions, and sometimes they operate like a well-oiled machine, enabling us to perform tasks and to deal with life most efficiently. Inheritance plays a vital part, of course, in how we function. And so, too, does environment — the neighborhood we live in, the atmosphere at home, the level of our education, the influence of religion. Each of us, then, is a bundle of interaction, heredity and environment working together to make us what we are and who we are.

There are times when one circumstance or the other — biological or environmental — seems to predominate. In such cases we might be able to blame one, or credit one, for something gone amiss or to our advantage. But more often than not we are a complex blend of nature and nurture that we have some degree of control over.

Consider for a moment the concept of free will, the faculty of making a reasonable selection from several choices. "Free will" does not necessarily mean we will always make the right choice, only that we can choose — if we want to, and are able to by virtue of a clear mind. Lecomte du Noüy, the respected biologist-philosopher who wrote in the 1940s, had this to say about free will:

> The negation of free will, the negation of moral responsibility; the individual considered merely as a physio-chemical unit, as a particle of living matter, hardly different from the other animals, inevitably brings about the death of man, the suppression of all spirituality, of all hope, the frightful and discouraging feeling of total uselessness. . . . It must be demonstrated that every man has a part to play and that he is free to play it or not; that he is a link in a chain and not a whisp of straw swept along by a torrent; that, in brief, human dignity is not a vain word, and that when a man is not convinced of this and does not try to attain this dignity, he lowers himself to the level of the beast.[1]

Not everyone agrees with the idea of free will. Among those who do not are the so-called determinists, individuals who believe that people don't really make choices at all, that everything that happens — including our choices — is caused by other events and occurs as a result of them.

There are, of course, things in our lives that we can do nothing or little about, and I do not want to convey the naive impression that we are the complete masters and mistresses of our lives. Disease and earthquakes and changes in the weather will come in their own time. We also will lose control and become angry on impulse, and insanely jealous when a girlfriend or boyfriend shows an interest in another. And we will give in, on occasion, to a temptation to smoke or to have sex indiscriminately or to drink too much, even though we have promised ourselves time and again that we will think a bit on the consequences before we do these things. We are after all only human, and human nature in the last analysis cannot be changed, only modified.

So, without plunging into a murky philosophical discussion of the issue, suffice it to say that *sometimes* our actions, as well as events, are determined, and *sometimes* they are free. Often, all it takes is a little thinking, a little time to deliberate, to weigh the alternatives and the consequences of each course of action.

We all have a responsibility for our own lives, then, and we can learn how to become responsible for much of what we do and for what happens to us, difficult as that may be to understand or actually to put into practice. Choices about how to conduct our lives are always being offered to us. There is no lack of them, you may be certain. What is important is that you make a choice, and that you make it because of your own values, not someone else's. Your choice will reveal your personal outlook on life to others, an outlook which, admittedly, will be tempered by your upbringing, religious beliefs, age, degree of maturity and experience.

Making a choice means taking charge of your life. One way to begin doing just that is to drop the idea that you have to please others on a regular basis, that you have to have their approval. People who always act the way others want them to act are not only putting tremendous pressure on themselves to conform to some behavioral standard not of their own choosing —they are also being dishonest with themselves. And dishonesty with self sooner or later will breed self-doubt and insecure feelings and, worse, dislike of self, which is one of the barriers to being considerate and loving to others.

Every one of us wants to be liked, to be wanted by others as friend or lover. And in an immensely popular book written more than forty years ago and still widely read, Dale Carnegie offered these six ways to achieve that goal:

1. Become genuinely interested in other people.
2. Smile.
3. Remember that a man's name is to him the sweetest and most important sound in any language.
4. Be a good listener. Encourage others to talk about themselves.
5. Talk in terms of the other's interest.
6. Make the other person feel important, and do it sincerely.[2]

This is sound advice. And it's probably true that the easiest way to be liked is to do all of the nice things that make us likable. But sometimes we overdo them. We bring gifts to people we want to impress with our generosity. We agree (when we really don't) with their points of view, be they political, religious or philosophical. We read and say we enjoy the same books the object of our attention enjoys, laugh at the same jokes, go to the same movies, even have sex when we don't really want to simply because it is what the other wants. If we act this way all the time, chances are we'll be surrounded with friends, or more aptly put, acquaintances who call themselves friends.

So convinced are we that no one would want us with all our warts and blemishes, we try to become someone we are not. We dishonestly put on a mask, a disguise that can be funny or tragic, depending on the situation and the person we want for a friend. But the longer we are dishonest with ourselves, the more insecure we become, because deep down inside there is the real person, the one we are ashamed of. And the more insecure we become, the more dependent we become on the approval of others. Our false face is rarely off now, and we get the approval we seek. We have a sense of identity — but it is a bogus one.

We now begin to cling to the person who appreciates us for the side we display. And soon, so intent are we on feeding our insecurity, that we neglect to notice the other's needs and desires — and in this sort of relationship, love dies. It may not, in fact, ever take root.

The problem with this kind of behavior is that no one ever gets to know the real you, the person who doesn't always want to pay for the hamburgers, or doesn't like the play or rock group that everyone else likes. The real you isn't necessarily all that bad. Not only are there an awful lot of people a good deal worse than you, but for you to believe that you aren't so hot means you're also willing to take someone else's word for it. Besides, there's a good possibility that when you put on an act, the very people you're trying to impress will see through it and whisper to a real friend later, "I can't stand people who are always trying to please." And if that's not enough reason to make you quit trying so hard to prove your worth, consider that the persons whose love you seek may not want you to be a mirror image of themselves, that quite possibly they might truly like the real you. The converse might also be true. That is, suppose your disguise is acceptable to someone else. And one day, as will surely happen, you drop the pose you have worked so hard to maintain. What will happen then to the love or the friendship based on the false face? What do you do when the music stops?

Dislike of oneself is a barrier to a loving relationship; and so is the parasitic dependency that stems from self-doubt, from our refusal or inability to establish our own true identity. It is true that people who like themselves are more readily liked, as are people who know how to blend correct amounts of honesty and charity and, just as important, who are considerate of others and capable of giving love.

But so that there will be no misunderstanding later on, a word or two should be said about the difference between self-love and selfishness, two states that ought not to be confused. Selfishness implies that people are motivated wholly by personal needs to the disregard of the well-being or desires of others. Selfish people find it difficult to share, whether it be a sandwich or a seat on a bus. They can't think of anyone but themselves when it comes to more intimate situations, like having sex. Selfish people cannot commit themselves — one of love's key ingredients — nor can they understand what the evangelist John meant when he said, "Greater love hath no man than this, that a man lay down his life for his friends." They wouldn't appreciate what it is that makes someone donate a kidney to save the life of a relative or friend, or give blood for a transfusion.

Self-love, on the other hand, is something positive. What it actually amounts to is being your own friend, secure in the knowledge that you are not perfect but not so bad after all. It means being free of the need to impress everyone in sight by behaving in a "likable" manner. Self-love means that you are *free* from being preoccupied with yourself. It means that you realize that being handsome or beautiful or wealthy, comforting though these externals may be, is not in itself the ticket to being liked. Normal self-love does not depend on the constant praise of others. The true narcissist — named after the youth in Greek legend who pined away for love of his own image as reflected in a pool — has a good deal of love for self but cannot feel that self-esteem without drawing on an overload of outside admiration and adulation. Psychologists argue that such individuals don't really love themselves at all. They may actually hold low opinions of themselves, and that is why they need so much attention. They are selfish, and this, of course, is a barrier to being able to give love.

Dr. Leo Buscaglia, an associate professor of education at the University of Southern California who developed a course on love, has put it nicely:

> To care about oneself is basic to love. Man loves himself when he sees himself with accuracy, genuinely appreciates what he sees, but is especially excited and challenged with the prospect of what he can become. . . . To love oneself is to struggle to rediscover and maintain your uniqueness. It is understanding and appreciating the idea that you will be the only you to ever live upon this earth, that when you die so will all of your fantastic possibilities. It is the realization

that even you are not totally aware of the wonders which lie dormant within yourself. . . . So loving yourself involves the discovery of the true wonder of you; not only the present you, but the many possibilities of you. It involves the continual realization that you are unique, like no other person in the world; that life is, or should be, the discovery, the development and the sharing of this uniqueness.[3]

Self-love, then, means having a sense of worth, having a storehouse of qualities that you yourself cherish. Psychologist George Weinberg refers to these as qualities so worthwhile to you that the people you really want for friends *ought* to like you for them. He advises that you work to develop these qualities for their own sake, for your own sake, without trying to impress anyone else.

It is, obviously, not easy to develop many of the qualities that make us like ourselves. In a lot of cases, it means actually re-engineering our personalities: forcing ourselves *not* to phone a friend because we're bored and can't stand being alone; becoming as quick to forgive as we are to anger; being genuinely happy and not envious when a friend wins a prize; avoiding the cynicism that tries to convince us that no one is ever honest and kind; learning how to enjoy life more; being able to disagree openly, particularly with someone we're afraid of losing.

Of this last, Weinberg says, "This is important in giving yourself a sense of purpose and identity. And it lets others know that you're capable of strong beliefs and strong feelings. It's hard to like anyone who isn't. Don't be a tag-along. If you are, you'll reinforce the doubt, 'What is there to like about me?' And that doubt will be partly right."[4]

Again, it is not easy. But rest assured that not everything is inevitable in this world, that most people are capable of emotional growth; and they do grow, because they believe they are responsible for their own lives, for their attitudes, and because they know which choices to make. Such people are not afraid to take chances. They don't have to hide under the soft comforter of familiarity, doing things because that's the way they've always been done or because others expect them to do things that way.

The ability to make choices means making bad ones as well as good ones. Consider, for a moment, *habit*. This is the tendency to repeat an action. Habit makes it easier for us to make difficult decisions. We do things because we have acquired the habit to do them. But, the problem is that we can choose to acquire nasty, even criminal habits, as well as correct ones, and we can just as proudly proclaim that we've exercised free will. In his *Summa Theologica,* Saint Thomas Aquinas points out that habit is a quality that lies between our powers to act and our acts. Our wills are capable of choosing to tell the truth, for example, but before we can choose to do so in any and all circumstances, we must acquire the habit of truthfulness.

We all hope, of course, that we won't choose the wrong road, and our reason for avoiding that road should not be because it might land us in jail. Decisions based on fear are not really decisions at all, and they are just as invalid as a confession beaten or tortured out of a prisoner. Remember that you have to like yourself, and it's not going to be easy to do that if you choose a way of behaving because you're made to. If you believe, as do most people, that human beings are basically honest, inclined toward truth, good and loyalty — although sometimes weak and easily sidetracked — then making your free choices from all the possibilities facing you and eventually slanting those choices in the "right" direction won't be too difficult.

The importance of commitment in love has been mentioned. This commitment involves being conscious of the other person's feelings, getting inside his or her skin, so to speak. If you stop and think, "How would I like it if he or she treated me that way?" before doing something that might offend, it will not only help you make the kind of decision that will make you likable in the end, but it will also be a demonstration of your ability to give affection. What it amounts to, in the simplest terms, is the Golden Rule: "Whatsoever ye would that men should do to you, do ye even so to them."

Being considerate of the other person is probably easiest when you're in the throes of the first stages of love, or, more precisely, when you're infatuated: that first overwhelming rush of feeling for another that arouses your body, races your heart, and quickens your breath. At this time, you don't see your mate's weaknesses and shortcomings, and it's a simple matter to "do unto others" when you know that what they'll do unto you is quite pleasant. It's at this time that Shakespeare's words truly apply: "Love is blind and lovers cannot see / The pretty follies that themselves commit." Is it any wonder that Cupid, the Roman god of love, is usually blindfolded?

But sooner or later lovers have to be honest. And when they do come down to earth, the world may not look so sunny. They begin to see things a bit more clearly. Their partners' moods begin to get on their nerves, and they say so, straight out. They might even become a bit dissatisfied with their partners.

One of the universal problems is that we're never satisfied. The grass is always greener, the familiar adage goes, in the other person's yard. That's true in a love relationship as well as in friendships. Often, we want whatever it is we cannot have. Professor Elaine Walster of the University of Wisconsin has addressed this issue, saying that many satisfied people day-dream about how permanently happy they would be if they had whatever it is they don't have. If either member of a couple encounters a new lover, for example, a person who promises to satisfy unfulfilled needs, he or she is likely to feel a strong stirring of emotions. "Such delightful encounters provide the fuel for new passionate experiences," says Walster. But the difficulty is that "as soon as the new lover begins to routinely satisfy these needs, new longings inevitably arise, and the search for a 'perfect' lover is on once again."[5]

We must be aware that this sort of thing is going to happen to all of us. The first stage of falling in love is somewhat irrational. But then will come a time when we must deal with the knight without his armor, with the princess without her veil of white. It is during this period of awakening that commitment becomes more important. Although it is not easy to do when you're in the middle of a passionate love affair, getting to know your partner really well — and that means more than physically — is essential. This means asking some of the same questions you ask about your friends. The answers will tell you much about yourself and help you to build a solid self-image. Observe your partner closely, not only when you're together but when you're with others. Find out how alike you are, how different, under certain circumstances. Ask yourself whether these similarities and differences will help or hinder the relationship. The science of magnetism may hold that unlike powers attract and like ones repel, but don't apply that rule now. Remember that you're dealing with a human being who has feelings, not with a piece of iron. The fact that someone is totally different from you doesn't have to mean he or she is meant for you. Nor does it mean you have to avoid someone who is just like you. Ask yourself why you're interested in the other person. Ask yourself why your mate is interested in you. Are you interested because he or she dresses beautifully, is well-groomed or sexy? Do you think your partner is interested in you because of the side you show? Is that side honest? Does family background have anything to do with it on either side? Is it your partner's "space-shot" personality? Or because he or she has come along at just the right time — your parents are on your back, you want the pressure off, you want a confidant?

If you read all of the signals right, and you're honest about the answers, then you've gotten to know yourself pretty well.

3

Homosexuality

Wʜᴇɴ ᴡᴇ ᴛᴀʟᴋ ᴀʙᴏᴜᴛ romantic love, we generally mean the deep feeling that binds a male and a female. Since Adam and Eve, cave man and cave woman, one has been attracted to the other, and it is not the purpose of this book to delve too deeply into the biological and psychological reasons behind that attraction. Let's just say that the passion between the sexes is necessary, and will remain so. As vice or virtue, you can count on its presence.

Most men are attracted to women, and women to men. There are, however, two exceptions to that state of affairs. The first is considered "normal," the other is not. I should point out here that the word *normal* means "conforming to a type or standard," and does not always imply mental imbalance or errant behavior. For example, what is considered normal drinking behavior in one culture might be seen as excessive by our society. And, to use another analogy, mental illness, we ought to understand that the problems of those we call mentally ill differ only in *degree* from the problems of those we know as normal. Whenever the word *normal* is used, always ask, "Compared to whom?"

The first exception to the universal attraction between males and females comes when we are children, or during adolescence, that period between childhood and adulthood. It is perfectly reasonable for young boys to prefer the company of other young boys, and young girls the company of young girls. Many also carry that preference to sexual intimacy, either as fantasy or in some sort of physical contact. The sexual feelings you may have had for members of your own sex during those years are by no means unusual, and probably most everyone, parents and grandparents included, has experienced them. This attraction becomes easier to understand when you consider that although your sex and your hereditary traits are determined at precisely the moment when a female egg cell is fertilized by a male sperm, the sexual characteristics that make you a male or a female — the testicles and the ovaries — do not appear until about the seventh week of pregnancy. In fact, we had the potential for both kinds of sexual characteristics in our gonads, the organs in which the reproductive cells develop, in the early stages of development. With the process known as *differentiation,* the gonads slowly begin to form either testes or ovaries, and other structures common to both males and females start to change into external genitals: the penis and scrotum in males, the vagina and clitoris in females. No matter what we become, however, male or female, we always carry with us some hint of our early bisexual (both-sexed) nature. Female genital organs contain vestiges of male structures, and the male breast has its nipples, which do not have the same function as those of a female but are there nevertheless.

The next exception to the usual situation of John prefers Jane, Jane prefers John is homosexuality. The homosexual male or female (the term for a homosexual woman is *lesbian*) is sexually attracted to members of his or her own sex. Such an individual's sex organs appear and function in the same way as those of heterosexuals, individuals who have the usual desire for members of the opposite sex. It is only the homosexuals' preference for members of their own sex that makes them different. A homosexual man can truly desire another man, a homosexual woman can desire another woman. Both male and female homosexuals may have sex with their partners, want only good for their loved ones, and wish to share their lives with them. In short, homosexuals can honestly feel committed love for one another, the same sort of love that man and woman feel for each other generally, a love that means involvement to the exclusion of other partners, with or without frequent sexual activity. The emotions they feel are genuine.

Somewhere along the way the homosexual did not develop the interest in members of the opposite sex that is the usual step for the adolescent who eventually loses his or her natural preference for members of the same sex.

There are some speculations about why people become homosexuals, and they'll be examined later. But consider another point first. That is that every one of us has a homosexual side — possibly a carry-over from those early fetal days when we had neutral sexual structures — no matter that we are men who love women or women who love men. Pauper, pope and prince, we are all bisexuals — that is, we can be attracted by both sexes. Again, it is a matter of degree, and many homosexuals are married to members of the opposite sex. Are you a homosexual if you are a young man who wants to spend a lot of time with a male friend, sharing a room together, going to movies and on drives together? Is the football player who spends so much time with his teammates, on and off the field, a homosexual? Is he more of one when he pats the right-end's rump after a neat pass-catch and a touchdown run? Is your father a homosexual if he kisses his brother? Is he more of one if the kiss is on the mouth? What about women? Are they homosexuals if they embrace and kiss and walk along the street arm in arm? Is your mother a homosexual if her only close friends are women? If a woman chooses not to marry, is homosexuality behind it? The middle-aged bachelor in your neighborhood who does not date — is he a homosexual?

Some of these people might, of course, be truly homosexual. But chances are that they are not. Millions of men and women have, however, had a sexual relationship with same-sex partners. According to estimates of the noted sex researcher Alfred C. Kinsey, male homosexuals make up about 4 percent of the U.S. population, female about 2 percent. These figures, however, refer to men and women who are exclusively homosexual — that is, who do not date members of the opposite sex at all.

Defining homosexuality adequately is a difficult task. What is certain is that an isolated sexual act with a member of the same sex does not necessarily mean either or both of the participants are homosexuals. Many men and women have at some time had sexually exciting physical contact with members of their own sex, sometimes to the point of orgasm. They are not considered true homosexuals by the psychiatrists and psychologists who have looked into the condition. For many years, real homosexuality — which means that the individual regularly chooses a member of the same sex as a sexual partner, as a lover — has been explained in numerous ways. It has been called learned

behavior, a personality disorder, a sexual deviation, a mental imbalance, a hormone-deficiency disease, and a moral weakness. In
1973, in a major shift in attitude, the American Psychiatric Association reversed a position it had held for nearly a hundred
years and declared that homosexuality is not a mental illness.
Instead, the organization of psychiatrists decided to define
homosexuality as a "sexual orientation disturbance." One of the
psychiatrists explained, "We're not saying that homosexuality
is either 'normal' or 'abnormal.' We're saying that homosexuality
per se is not a psychiatric disorder."

The traditional view among psychiatrists that homosexuality
is an emotional illness — a view still held by many despite the
psychiatric association's stand — is coupled with the belief that
its only effective treatment is psychotherapy. A "cure," then,
would mean that the homosexual is converted to heterosexual
behavior — with a preference for members of the opposite sex.

In a report some years ago in the *Journal of the American
Medical Association,* Dr. Charles W. Socarides of the Albert Ein-
stein College of Medicine noted that homosexuality is learned,
acquired behavior. It is not, he said, innate or instinctual. He
disagreed that homosexuality should be granted acceptance as
a valid form of sexual functioning, different from but equal to
heterosexuality. Equally misleading, said Dr. Socarides, was the
idea that homosexuality is merely an aspect of normal development, a transient stage of adolescence. His definition of a homosexual was that of a person who consistently and from inner
necessity engages in homosexual acts. "This pattern arises from
faulty sexual identity, a product of the earliest years of life," he
explained. "Typically, we find a pathological family constella-
tion in which there is a domineering, crushing mother who will
not allow the developing child to achieve autonomy from her,

and an absent, weak or rejecting father."[1] Note the parallel here with the aforementioned studies that demonstrated the adverse effect of a flawed parent-child relationship on the subsequent behavior of the offspring.

Not everyone agrees with the idea that an overprotective mother and an unaffectionate father are the reasons why some individuals become homosexual. A few years ago, a Loma Linda University psychologist, Dr. Ray B. Evans, challenged that widely held theory, saying that while childhood parental relationships of many homosexuals appear less desirable than those of heterosexuals, the observation does not establish a causal connection. The notion that a particular son becomes homosexual because of a mother who is close-binding and intimate with him, and a detached or hostile father, was given impetus by a 1962 study by a group of psychoanalysts headed by Dr. Irving Bieber of New York Medical College. The analysts felt that the parents' relationship with the homosexual son differed from their relationship with other children and was determined largely by the parents' own unresolved problems.

But, said Dr. Evans, it may be that the quality of the relationship with the son is different because that son is different. "Obviously, children are affected by the kind of parents they have, but parents are also influenced by their children, and the relationship between them does not emanate from the parents alone," he reported in 1971 in the journal *Medical Aspects of Human Sexuality*.

It is just as tenable to assume that the father of a prehomosexual son becomes detached or hostile because he does not understand his son, is disappointed in him, or threatened by him, as it is to assume that the son becomes homosexual because of the father's rejection. Similarly, it is as reasonable to assume that a mother becomes intimate and close-binding with her potentially homosexual son because of the kind of person he is as to assume he becomes homosexual because she is too binding and intimate with him.

In a more recent study involving homosexual women, a team of researchers at the Postgraduate Center for Mental Health in New York City checked into the background of some two hundred lesbians and about the same number of nonhomosexual women. After examining each group's family relationships and sexual development, the researchers concluded that it was difficult to find any conspicuous factors that would set the female homosexuals apart from the nonhomosexuals. The researchers tested the women further in an effort to determine their emotional reactions to the concepts of mother, father, man, woman, friend and lover. Again, said a report on the study in *The Sciences,* they found no clear-cut evidence of any differences between the experimental groups.

"We cannot document significant pathology running through all homosexual women," Dr. Bernard Riess, one of the researchers, observed. "They do not differ noticeably in their pre-adult experiences and family patterns from heterosexual women. Also, it is hard to describe anyone as a homosexual female because there are so many different kinds of homosexual relationships. Some of the women [studied] are single, some are married, some live in pairs. Almost all have been bisexual."[2]

In challenging the old cliché about homosexual men and domineering mothers, the above-mentioned Evans study suggested an alternative hypothesis. Perhaps the man who becomes a homosexual is born with a genetic, biological or biochemical difference from other men. Evans speculated that perhaps certain environmental factors also are necessary in addition to a biological predisposition — but, in his opinion, the particular experiences necessary for the development of homosexuality have not been verified.

In recent years, the idea that biological factors — notably hormones — are at work in homosexuality has caught on among some researchers. One noteworthy investigation was conducted by physicians at the New England Deaconess Hospital in Boston and at Washington University School of Medicine in Saint Louis. Their work, reported in the *New England Journal of Medicine,* challenged the suggestion that the "disorder" is brought on by environmental factors, particularly the father-mother role. The investigators compared thirty male homosexuals with a control group of fifty heterosexuals. They found that the homosexuals had sharply lower levels of the male hormone testosterone in their blood. (Testosterone, produced by the male sex glands, is responsible for such male characteristics as a deep voice and hair growth, and also for the function of certain reproductive organs.)

The thirty homosexuals studied by Dr. Robert C. Kolodny and his colleagues were volunteers, college students between the ages of eighteen and twenty-four. All were unmarried and in good academic standing. Two-thirds of the men recalled happy childhoods and more than two-thirds saw their father as the dominant parent. It should be made clear that none of the studies thus far has established a solid hormonal basis for homosexuality, and Dr. Kolodny's team cautioned that the results have to be interpreted carefully because of the small number of subjects. But while the group did not suggest that hormonal imbalances would turn up in the great majority of homosexuals, it did emphasize that such a connection has to be considered. Even famed sex researchers William Masters and Virginia Johnson, who believe that homosexuality is learned — "One learns it from one's peers, one learns it from one's family, one learns it at school, everywhere," Masters remarked recently — have acknowledged that an open mind must be kept on the matter. "In view of the current lack of secure information in this field," they observed in a new book on homosexuality, "we must maintain an intellectually open stance acknowledging that in at least some instances — though clearly not in most cases — hormonal predispositions may interact with social and environmental factors to lead toward a homosexual orientation."[3]

Regardless of the lack of concrete evidence and the differences of opinion over cause, psychiatrists try to deal with the homosexuals who seek their help. The methods used — and these may include drug treatment, psychoanalysis, group therapy, behavior modification, even brain surgery — have as their goal a complete return to sexual drives that are considered normal by society. Sometimes treatment works, but often it does not and many therapists have admitted a failure rate of 80 percent. (In their recent report, Masters and Johnson claimed that they helped 151 homosexuals turn to heterosexuality, with only a 35 percent failure rate. Some sex-behavior researchers have challenged this, saying that the two researchers might not have been studying homosexuals at all, but bisexuals or even maladjusted heterosexuals.)

In discussing treatment, psychiatrists sometimes emphasize the need to guide very young children onto a normal sexual path, reasoning that the earlier symptoms are recognized, the better the hope for lasting change. Often, this approach means that parents must not interfere unduly with a child's interest in

and activities with the opposite sex, and that they should try
to reinforce masculine traits in their young sons, and feminine
ones in their young daughters. This does not mean that girls
should be encouraged to be secretaries and teachers, and boys
groomed for positions as doctors or lawyers or mechanics. Nor
does it mean that boys should never cuddle a teddy bear, nor
girls play football.

An emphasis of that sort is known as *misdirected gender
orientation*. You probably know it as sexism, or chauvinism,
and it is the sort of thing that has led to all of the injustices
women have been subjected to, on the job and in their social
lives. It is also what conditions a man not to show tenderness
in public. The proper reinforcement of gender traits means re-
minding boys and girls that they are males and females, similar
in feelings and desires and abilities, yet different in significant
biological ways and roles. (We cannot take the time here to
discuss the differences between men and women. The subject
is debated continually by behavioral scientists, and while the
physical differences are fairly obvious, the psychological ones,
when they exist, are not always. Suffice it to say that the potential for being a mother or a father, the unique nature of the sex
hormones, and how much we imitate our fathers and mothers,
or are encouraged to do so, all play a major part in making us
behave in the ways that are special to our sex. We do not live in
a neuter world, no matter what some hair stylists, clothing
designers and other sex-erasers would have us believe. For
underneath the jeans and the unisex hair is a man or a woman
— although sometimes, as we have said, something goes askew
with that sexual identity.)

Despite the fact that many psychiatrists feel that reverting to
heterosexuality is the only logical step for homosexuals, many

homosexuals simply do not wish to change. They resent any suggestion that they are "sick." Their preference, they believe, is as acceptable a form of behavior as heterosexuality. And they have asked that the courts and the community recognize this.

Some homosexuals keep silent about their preference, and few of their neighbors know about it. More and more, however, homosexuals are declaring their choice publicly, "coming out of the closet," as they put it. And so we read in the news about Dr. Howard Brown, a member of the faculty at New York University and once New York City's health commissioner. He revealed his homosexuality, he said, to help free future generations "from the dreadful agony of secrecy, the constant need to hide." There was Harvey Milk, the first avowed homosexual to be elected to San Francisco's Board of Supervisors. "If a gay can win," he declared, "it means there is hope that the system can work for all minorities if they fight. If I do a good job, people won't care if I'm green or if I have three heads." (Milk's story took a tragic turn in 1978. He was murdered, along with Mayor George Moscone, in the San Francisco City Hall.)

Sometimes, openness doesn't hurt. Recently, a New York Methodist minister who publicly acknowledged being a homosexual was allowed to continue as pastor of his church. "I have a briefcase full of letters from members of the church, supporting him," said the chairman of the ministerial board, "and I don't have a single one that's negative."

For others, however, the honest road is a difficult one to walk. Elaine Noble, a Massachusetts State Representative and the first admitted lesbian to be elected to state office, had her share of problems. She lost her job with an advertising agency, her female lover — who feared being seen with her — and, as Noble put it, "at least for a time, a certain portion of my sanity." She had to suffer obscene phone calls, and her car tires were slashed. There were problems, too, for Thomas P. Sweetin, a candidate for the Jesuit priesthood in New York. Sweetin was dismissed by the order after being told he would be denied ordination because he was an admitted homosexual. "It is true, I am a homosexual," he wrote in his appeal. "However, I have never once acted upon my homosexuality, nor have I ever attempted to justify anyone's acting upon his or her sexuality." The difference in his case, he added, was not that he was homosexual, but that he was willing to openly acknowledge his feelings and his belief that there was nothing in those feelings to be ashamed of.

Other homosexuals have requested that they be allowed to marry members of their sex in church, and a number of ceremonies have been performed by gay ministers. Such activities were characterized by one Vatican theologian as "simply moral aberrations that cannot be approved by human conscience, much less Christian conscience." Consecrating a union between two people of the same sex, he went on, was sanctioning a "totally and radically revolutionary concept" outside all laws, social systems and ethical customs.

When homosexuals are not "coming out" singly, they may do so as members of organizations, among them the Gay Liberation Front, the Mattachine Society, the Student Homophile League, the Gay Activists Alliance, Gay Vietnam Veterans, and Dignity, a group of Catholic homosexuals. Such groups, their members feel, will help win community acceptance of their cause and dispel some of the many myths about homosexuality. The acceptance, however, is not easily won.

Homosexuality, whether it is seen as a medical disorder or a way of life, remains an emotion-filled issue. Many people still have difficulty discussing the subject and, when they do, it is usually in outrage. Think of the times you yourself have referred to certain people — boys who avoid physical fights or who play with girls, girls who climb telephone poles and compete with boys — in crude terms like "faggot," "fag," "fairy," "queer," "fruit," "butch," "dyke." You have probably heard the expression "overt" homosexual — meaning one who consciously recognizes and practices homosexuality. Or, you might hear whispers about an unmarried priest or a neighbor as a "latent" homosexual — one who has unconscious homosexual desires. You have also heard or read about Anita Bryant, the singer and promoter of orange juice who has vehemently opposed homosexuality and led a successful movement recently to repeal a law in Dade County, Florida, that banned discrimination against homosexuals. When voters in Saint Paul, Minnesota, repealed a similar rights law, Bryant commented, "The morally committed majority has won a great victory. And the message is clear. No longer will God-respecting Americans submit to militant, politically organized immorality."

Public opinion polls have demonstrated time and again that the majority of U.S. citizens feel homosexuals ought to be punished for homosexual acts, even though they are performed in private, and believe that homosexuality is more detrimental to society than adultery. "I'm certain that my dad would be more upset if he found out I were living with a lesbian than if I were raped by some madman," a young woman friend told me. "He can easily understand a man performing a sex act with a woman, violent or not."

The law, in fact, is quite hard on homosexuals. In a majority of the states, sodomy (sexual intercourse between males) is illegal and may be punished by heavy prison sentences. Some cities have successfully barred homosexuals from buying or renting homes, and there are any number of cases of discrimination against homosexuals in the business, professional and academic worlds. The military services have traditionally released homosexuals with a "less than honorable" discharge, and a homosexual would still find it difficult to obtain a security clearance for employment with the CIA or FBI. In 1975, the case of Air Force Sergeant Leonard Matlovich, a decorated Vietnam veteran, made headlines. Matlovich told his superiors he was homosexual and became involved in a lengthy battle to prevent the Air Force from forcing him out of the service. The sergeant, whose story was the subject of a nationally televised drama, lost his court fight to stay on his job, one that he had handled admirably. He could have remained in the service if he had not made his sexual preference public. But, as he said, "I will not live a lie."

On the other side of it, a number of communities have adopted laws that specifically ban discrimination because of sexual preference. In New York City, one of the first actions Mayor Koch took after he assumed office was to issue an order forbidding discrimination against homosexuals by city agencies and officials. The mayor's move drew the following retort from Samuel DeMilia, president of the Patrolmen's Benevolent Association:

The hastily issued order will be unworkable in the Police Department, and can do more harm than good. The Mayor is in effect trying a social experiment in the very sensitive area of public safety, and the results to department morale and performance can be catastrophic. . . . The overt homosexual is distinguished by his speech, mannerisms, conduct and dress. These have generally been received negatively by the public. There is no reason to believe that public attitudes will change once he puts on a police officer's uniform. [According to the *New York Times,* undocumented allegations put the number of homosexuals in the New York Police Department as high as five thousand.][4]

The California Supreme Court has also sided against discrimination. It ruled that homosexuality is no reason for disqualifying a schoolteacher (a view not shared by many parents and school committees who regard homosexuals as a bad influence, regardless of their qualifications as teachers). The District of Columbia School Board has taken a similar stand on the side of homosexuals. In a 1971 immigration case, a Federal District Court judge in New York City ruled that an applicant for U.S. citizenship should not be discriminated against because he was a homosexual. The judge ruled in the case of a twenty-four-year-old homosexual from Cuba whose application for citizenship was opposed by the U.S. Immigration and Naturalization Service. The young man, the judge said, had never bothered anyone, had not corrupted anyone's morals, and had confined his sexual preference to consenting adults, in private. "We accept the principle that the naturalization laws are concerned with public, not private, morality," the judge ruled.

With regard to the dropping of other barriers against hiring homosexuals, *Time* magazine reported in 1975:

Some major corporations, including American Telephone & Telegraph, the Bank of America, IBM, and NBC, have declared themselves equal-opportunity employers with regard to homosexuals. Honeywell, which publicly refused to hire gays in 1970, lifted the ban seven months before Minneapolis, where its home office is located, passed an anti-discrimination ordinance in 1974. Most significantly, the Federal Civil Service Commission reversed its ruling that gays are unfit for public service. About 90 percent of the nation's 2.6 million federal civilian employees are covered by the new policy.[5]

But despite the pockets of awareness that the homosexual has rights as a human being — rights to respect, justice and everything that heterosexuals take for granted — the homosexual man or woman is probably still, in the words of Michael Brown, founder of the Gay Liberation Front, a member of the most persecuted, harassed minority group in history. Some of this harassment is based on the fear of many parents and psychologists that too much emphasis on the issue might adversely affect the very young whose sexual identities have not yet fully developed.

Reinforcing appropriate sexual traits, as suggested earlier, is important for healthy, normal emotional growth. But much of the ill feeling aimed at homosexuals is grounded in myths and misconceptions, in strong definitions of "normal" and "abnormal," and in a morality that stretches back to the days when humans first began keeping records. "If any one lie with a man as well as with a woman, both have committed an abomination, let them be put to death," the Bible's Book of Leviticus proclaims. In the First Epistle of Saint Paul to the Corinthians, effeminate persons and "liers with mankind" are included along with fornicators, adulterers and idolators, who can never possess the kingdom of God.

The early Romans and Greeks were both tolerant and critical of homosexuality at various periods in their history, and there are many references in their literature both denouncing the practice as immoral and singing its praises. Aristotle attributed the popularity of homosexual acts to fear of overpopulation, and Plato, who once wrote a dialogue in which guests at a banquet speak in honor of love, mainly between males, later condemned homosexual practices as against nature.

Closer to our own time, there was the celebrated case of Oscar Wilde (1854–1900), the Irish-born poet, dramatist and novelist. During Wilde's undergraduate years at Oxford, he became the leader of an "art for art's sake" movement. He wore his hair long, dressed in bizarre clothes, and held flowers in his hand while lecturing. Caricatured in Gilbert and Sullivan's comic opera *Patience,* Wilde was eventually accused of homosexual practices, tried, and found guilty. He was sentenced to hard labor in prison, and after his release he moved to Paris where, under the assumed name of Sebastian Melmoth, he died a bitter and despairing man.

If insinuations and charges that homosexuals are all sinners or criminals can begin to be ignored, we can move on to dispelling some of the other stereotypes about this group of men and women. The first one you ought to forget is that male homosexuals are all painted and perfumed "swishy" dancers with feminine voices, and that lesbians are aggressive females who always wear pants and speak in gruff tones. Remember that how people dress and sound, or the sort of work they do, are not always good indicators of what they're like. Soldiers, professional football players and policemen can be homosexual. So, too, are some very feminine-appearing women.

True, some homosexuals do fit the stereotype, but they are in the minority. Very recently, a major new study on homosexuality was released by the Institute for Sex Research founded by Dr. Alfred Kinsey. In preparation since 1967 and based on interviews with some fifteen hundred "gays" and "straights" (the latter meaning nonhomosexuals) in the San Francisco area, the study found, among other things, that fewer than 10 percent of the homosexual men were employed in what are considered prime jobs for homosexuals: hairdressing, decorating, designing and dancing. Another popular conception — that homosexuals are madly driven by sex and that they are unstable, guilt-ridden individuals — was also shot down. According to the study, which was commissioned by the National Institute of Mental Health, while some homosexuals do resemble the usual conception, others act just like married heterosexuals. Instead of lumping homosexuals into one large group, the investigators, Drs. Alan B. Bell and Martin S. Weinberg, categorized them as several different types. These included the following: *close-couples,* who live as married people, contented and sexually faithful to each other; *open-couples,* who tend to be less dependent on each other but are less satisfied and seek outside sexual contact, and have more regrets about being homosexual; *functionals,* homosexuals who live as "swinging singles," cruising gay bars for partners, confident, and with few sexual problems; *dysfunctionals,* single and sexually active but with regrets about their homosexuality and not as confident about themselves; *asexuals,* who are older, not sexually active and more secretive, and who have a good deal of regret about their condition.

The study came up with a number of other interesting facts. One was that male homosexuals had developed closer friendships than male heterosexuals, and that the men in the close-couple arrangement were happier than heterosexuals. Another was that only about 75 percent of the men and 50 percent of the women considered themselves exclusively homosexuals, and a third of the women and a fifth of the men had been married to members of the opposite sex.

Commented Dr. Bell: "The report shows that homosexuality is not *ipso facto* pathological and that all homosexuals cannot be lumped together."

But despite all this, it is still not easy to love as a homosexual. "My lover and I are still afraid to go out together for a beer or for dinner," a gay New York City police officer wrote in an anonymous letter to the *New York Times*.

> We're afraid of being seen together. It's very painful when he's excluded from police department functions, like my promotions (and I've had many promotions). My colleagues bring wives and kids to share their honor. I've always been alone and I guess it's likely to be that way. But I'd like nothing better than one day to have my lover pick me up in the car after work and have my fellow officers call out . . . "Hey, your lover's here," as matter-of-factly as they do, "Hey, Reilly, your wife's here."[6]

Homosexuality has been with us since the dawn of history; that should have been long enough to soften its shock. But that's not the way it is, and it may well be that society will never accept it, no matter how many homosexuals come out, or how many gay rallies and marches are held.

In the end, you must ask whether homosexuals are injuring *you* by their actions, whether they are violating *your* civil rights, whether they are lurking behind every bush and in every public washroom, ready to leap at you and lead you into a life of sexual immorality.

It is important to understand that homosexuals do not fit one stereotype, one mold, and that they do not all become homosexuals for the same reasons. They are as different in their attitudes toward sex as any group of heterosexuals are. Some are promiscuous, and the rate of venereal disease among homosexuals who have numerous sex partners is high. But we cannot ignore the fact that most homosexuals want just what most of us want: warm relationships, someone special who cares, an opportunity to live and work as they choose, understanding. It is good for us to remember that while we might argue that homosexuality is wrong, or not for us, our criticism ought to focus on the condition, not on condemning the person who is caught up in it.

4

Jealousy

WHEN'S THE LAST TIME you were jealous? I don't mean the sort of jealousy that gnawed at you when one of your classmates got a new car for graduation. That's more appropriately called envy, and it's the desire to have something possessed by another. Chances are, that kind of feeling won't hang on too long, and it usually goes away when your classmate drives off into the sunset.

I'm speaking of the other kind of jealousy, the kind you'd experience if your classmate drove off into the sunset with your lover. This kind comes from a fear of losing something you already have. It will last longer, and it's what Iago meant when he told Othello, "O, beware, my lord, of jealousy. It is the green-eyed monster."

It is that, and more. Grounded as it is on real or suspected loss, jealousy is one of the most destructive of human emotions. Schiller, the German poet and philosopher, called it a "magnifier of trifles," and the Bible refers to it as the "rage of man." John Dryden, the English dramatist, knew it as the "jaundice of the soul." Today, psychologists define jealousy as a complex emotional state involving hatred of one person for another because of the relationship of both to a third. Sexual jealousy is by far the most common form. And the irony of it is that it stems — with all of its resentment and distress and hatred — from so positive an emotion as love. It can come from loving too much, too possessively. It is a price that love, unfortunately, exacts too often.

When we love deeply, it is natural for us to want to hold on to the one we love. So, when someone else intrudes into the relationship (again, that intrusion may be real or imagined), and our love object begins to show signs of cutting out in favor of a change, we react by being jealous.

There are many kinds and degrees of jealousy. You might, for instance, feel just a little twinge of it when your girlfriend or boyfriend merely looks twice at another. But you're able to shake it off, and it passes. Other times, the jealous feeling may be so strong that it prevents you from studying or working.

But mild or severe, jealousy hurts — and not only the person who is jealous. Take, for example, the girl whose boyfriend chooses to go bowling with someone else of the opposite sex because she's busy with family or with schoolwork. Her immediate response is anger. Next, she sulks, pitying herself, convinced that her lover doesn't care about her at all and is doing exactly what she's always known he would do. She expresses all of these feelings and suspicions to her boyfriend the next day, and she gets one of two responses. Her partner may feel extremely guilty over the bowling date and do everything possible to soothe her, even promising never to do it again. Or, he may become resentful of her attempt to manipulate and control his life. That resentment, that strong feeling of indignant displeasure, is the same as the emotion you express when you are jealous, and it is just as real, just as destructive of the relationship. So, too, is the guilt that you may instill in your partner. Jealousy, then, can be a no-win emotion.

Remember what was said earlier about dishonesty, putting on a false face to make someone like you? Making someone feel guilty is forcing them, in many instances, to be dishonest. The girl's boyfriend went to the bowling alley because he wanted to, and he was being honest about his feelings. Maybe he really liked being with that other person. If so, that's something the girl has to deal with separately. The point, though, is that making her boyfriend feel sorry for something he's probably not really sorry about — the only thing he's sorry about is that she's angry — is forcing him to pose. The soothing words he offers her, the flowers or the other gifts that will come later if she persists in playing the wounded swan, are but exaggerated responses to her carrying on. Her antics are emotional blackmail; they are very much like asking someone for a present instead of waiting for one to be given spontaneously.

Some people have suggested that jealousy is learned and has nothing to do with our biological makeup. George and Nena O'Neill, a husband-and-wife anthropological team who a few years ago wrote a best-selling book, *Open Marriage*, have observed:

To begin with, we would like to lay to rest the idea that sexual jealousy is natural, instinctive and inevitable. It is none of these things. Jealousy is primarily a *learned* response, determined by cultural attitudes. In many societies around the world, including the Eskimo, the Marquesans, the Lobi of West Africa, the Siriono of Bolivia and others, jealousy is at a minimum; and in still others, such as the Toda of India, it is almost completely absent. If in other societies it is greatly reduced or hardly exists at all, then it cannot be regarded as "natural" to man's behavior.[1]

But think about it yourself. Again, when you really like someone it's understandable for you to become upset if he or she starts paying more attention to someone else. All the advice in the world about gritting your teeth and bearing it and taking that other person's interest in your boyfriend or girlfriend as a compliment to your taste and good fortune isn't going to stop the wave of jealousy from hitting you. It will wash over you and, in most cases, will subside. There is an adage that tells us that the person who loves without jealousy does not truly love.

Putting personal observations aside for the moment, let's look at what's behind jealous responses and, although we're probably not going to be able to wipe it out, at how we might make it easier to handle.

How is it possible to deal with this strong, negative emotion? Dr. Gordon Clanton, a sociologist at San Diego State University, and Dr. Lynn Smith, a California social psychologist, point out that it is important to ask if a particular experience of jealousy comes from feeling excluded, or from a fear of loss. The distinction, they believe, is important because it spells the difference between a small problem and a large one.

"Most jealous flashes come from feeling left out of an activity involving your partner and another person or other people," Clanton and Smith say. "When your partner pays attention to another, your first reaction is to note that they are 'in' and you are 'out.' They are not noticing you, or at least not giving you as much attention as they are giving each other. You feel excluded, ignored, unappreciated."[2]

This kind of feeling is not uncommon. Your partner wants to dance with someone else at a party. Or your partner spends more time in conversation in another part of the room than you think he or she should. You're not a sports fan, but your partner finds someone who is. Such experiences, according to Clanton and Smith, trigger the jealous flash, but typically do not fan it into a flame. However, they add, if you find yourself troubled or upset by having to share your partner in ways normally considered appropriate among your friends, your feeling of being left out may be a sign of an underlying fear of loss — of the partner and of the love, affection and support he or she provides. This is the more serious kind of jealousy.

"This can be terrifying," say the two researchers. "And not surprisingly, you become anxious and defensive. You assume on questionable grounds that if you lose your mate it will be to someone else, so you view others with suspicion and fear. Such behavior makes you less attractive to your partner. Thus jealousy begets the very aloofness one suspects, and thereby deepens the basic fear of loss that leads to increased jealousy."[3]

What to do about it?

It was said earlier that when you like yourself you are more readily liked and are more considerate of others, and thus capable of giving love. It was said also that self-love means not that you are preoccupied with yourself but that you have a deep sense of self-worth and qualities that make you like yourself. Insofar as jealousy is concerned, chances are that when you feel good about yourself you are not as likely to feel jealous. This is so, say Clanton and Smith, because your jealousy, no matter the type, is shaped in part by elements such as your mood. "When you are depressed and dissatisfied with yourself, you are more susceptible. When you feel secure in your relationship, jealousy is less apt to be a problem. When you are unhappy or unsure about the relationship, you will be more fearful. Your feelings about the third party are also important. If you like and consider him or her a worthy friend for your partner, their occasional affectionate hugs may not bother you. If you don't, the same gestures may be unsettling and even threatening."[4]

One of the best ways to ward off jealousy's stabs is to bolster your image of yourself by trying to lessen your feelings of insecurity. Since you are a special person, you ought to work on developing the qualities that might make you even more individual. Instead of taking a course in medieval literature (unless, of course, you really want to) because your partner is into the subject, why not become more proficient in the subject or activities that you feel good about? What it all comes down to is broadening your horizons, doing something well by taking advantage of what you have to work with. When you do things like that — it may be joining an explorer's club or learning a trade or becoming an expert clam digger — you'll have much to say on those occasions when you're with people who seem to have it all going for them. You won't feel left out, and best of all you won't be fearful that everyone in the room is special but you, or that your partner always seems to find others more interesting. Jealousy (and envy) can't thrive if you fulfill yourself.

Closely tied to developing the strengths that will help stamp out insecurity is independence. This doesn't only mean that you learn to do things on your own without having to please another. It also means that you allow your partner independence of his or her own. It means learning to let go so that both you and your partner will have the necessary freedom to move about, to try new things, to grow. The main point is that if you're not able to quit being one half of a matched pair you're going to have a hard time when your partner decides there are some things he or she wants to do alone. Sharing is, of course, an important element in a relationship. This does not mean, however, that we ought to do everything together, go everywhere together, have the same friends, like the same music and so on. Why does a relationship have to be a tandem bike ride? It doesn't, and there is no reason why each of you shouldn't pursue whatever it is you want to pursue, independent of the other.

You'll probably welcome the opportunity to do things on your own, once you try it. And the more time you devote to getting to know yourself, the better off you'll be in the long run. You'll have learned to live with yourself, the first step toward learning to live with someone else. Togetherness is pleasant and important. But there are times, more than most people realize, when it can be oppressive, destructive and, in the context of what we are discussing here, the fertilizer that makes jealousy grow. The more possessive you become of your partner, the more injured you will feel when he or she announces the need to make a trip without you, or shows an interest in someone else who fills a need you cannot. This leads back to the point made earlier, and that is that you'd have to be superhuman to be all things to your friend. No one can ever be that, no matter how close and how good the relationship. The reason, as indicated before, is that you, and everyone else, are special. You and your partner may think alike in many ways, even most of the time, but there will come a time when your own special desires will show themselves. They may even be desires that you've hidden for a long time because you were afraid of damaging the relationship. They may be desires that you've only just become aware of. Or there may be things about you that someone, not your current steady partner, has just begun to notice. That new person likes those qualities in you and wants you for a friend because of them. The same holds true for you. You may meet someone new who shares an interest. Whatever the circumstances, it is important, as we said when discussing friendship, that you cultivate different people for different reasons, and that you don't avoid doing so out of some misguided idea that you already have a partner who answers all your needs.

When you feel comfortable with all of this, when you don't see a thing wrong with liking someone for one quality and someone else for another, you'll have gone a long way toward learning how to have a mature and happy relationship. Moreover, you'll come to understand that your feeling for another doesn't have to mean you love your current partner any less. Or, for that matter, that your partner loves you any less because he or she has other interests. It should never come down to an either-or situation — that is, you telling your partner, "Look, if you so much as look at another guy/girl again, you can forget about me." If you remember that the one you love is special to you in more ways than the limited ways in which others are special to you, and you always keep your real partner first, then you won't have to worry about damaging the relationship.

A young friend of mine sums it all up this way:

A secure individual trusts his or her lover and their love. Panic does not set in when he or she is absent, nor will the secure individual worry if their partner has unshared friends or activities. A basic belief in one's own self-worth and lovableness allows people to be confident in the face of separation, whether daily or monthly. The ability to put a lover's needs and desires ahead of our own allows us to let love go. If one person needs room to grow and move about the world more independently, or seeks expanding horizons of school, employment, even new love, then the truly loving person lets them go. When we love someone absolutely, we want what is best for him or her, not for ourselves. We try not to worry about what *I* shall do without *you,* but only that you succeed in finding happiness. Each of us, as long as we work at becoming whole people, will still be able to stand on our own two feet.

Communication, that other dimension of loving, comes in here too. It means the ability to make yourself known to another. This includes conveying, verbally and nonverbally, with words or a touch or a look, your concern and understanding, your needs and expectations. Some people are unable to do this. A young man might hide behind a macho mask, believing that to show tenderness or remorse is a sign of femininity. A young woman might avoid communicating because she doesn't want to bare feelings that will show her insecurities and leave her vulnerable. Some people transmit distorted messages, and when the transmission is garbled there can be no understanding of one another, least of all of any problems at hand. Such individuals argue a lot and the anger they display makes jealousy and the other negative emotions worse.

One thing to remember about communicating is that to be effective it must be as honest as possible. You can't ever assume that your partner knows what you're thinking all the time. Eventually, you'll have to discuss the things that trouble you about your relationship. You'll have to discuss the things you like about it. Sometimes, when you see that your partner is interested in another, maybe a more attractive, person, you may feel that it's because you are nothing. Your self-worth drops into the pits, and jealousy leaps out. Talk about it. Talk about whether you recall feeling that your mother liked your brother or sister more than you. Maybe some friend used to kid you about your long nose, or about your extra-small breasts or the funny way you laugh. So often, the way others have seen you as a sexual object affects your self-esteem. You have to get that out in the open, mention it to your partner. Learn to talk to yourself every so often, too. Ask yourself whether you're jealous because you're afraid of losing your mate, or because you feel left out. Make up some "jealousy" situations involving you, your partner and other people. Ask them all if they'd like to be included in a discussion, then try to find out what each would do in the situations outlined. Try to determine why each would react the way he says he would.

Dorothy Barash, a family therapist at the Menninger Foundation's Center for Applied Behavioral Sciences, writes: "Emotions such as frustrations, hurt, anger and disappointment which are not communicated and resolved, can be repressed so effectively over a long period of time that they are no longer identifiable. Incident after incident may be pushed down to become a deep, undefined emotional sore." Barash feels that one cannot change what has happened in the past, that is, disagreements and conflicts that have been smoldering for some time. But, she says, we can try to understand it. "We can free long-repressed rage and resentment by talking about it, acknowledging the hurts and feelings the [other] may not have known about. The process of talking over the hurt and being listened to, and perhaps finally feeling understood, is a form of catharsis which in itself is therapeutic. Once the past is looked at, a communication block is often removed. Then renegotiations can take place with the task of exploring vital questions. Where do we go from here?"[5]

It's important that you learn to listen, too, that you draw people out by showing interest. As the Greek philosopher Diogenes put it, "We have two ears and only one tongue in order that we may hear more and speak less." Communicating effectively means being a good listener as well as a good talker, and it's probably the best way to learn. Your partner tells you he or she needs more privacy and why. Or it may be that he or she wants to date other people once in a while. Rather than cut your partner off before the words are out, listen and try to understand. Chances are if that person is honest with you you'll find it more difficult to be angry than if he or she were deceitful.

But, a word of caution about communicating. Being honest doesn't mean being totally truthful; it doesn't mean you have to lay bare your every thought and feeling and desire. And it doesn't mean you should be unwrapping every single part of your friend's psyche, either. We all need to maintain some degree of privacy, if only to make us a bit more interesting, if only to keep others guessing a little about us. Once in a while, look at yourself as a pool of still, quiet water in a noisy world. The advice "Let it all hang out" may be fine for some people, but as a practical matter, it's better to hold back just enough to keep the communication channels clear of potentially harmful messages. Honesty may well be the best policy in business and moral affairs, but too much of it can be as harmful to a relationship as too little. You'll have to decide how much communication is too much. Bluntly telling your boyfriend or girlfriend that you're attracted to another because the new person is more intelligent or sexier is as cruel as it is foolish. You may well be telling the truth, but I doubt seriously that it will help the situation. It is best, always, to temper the truth with charity, that virtue of the heart, of lenient judgment, of which Saint Paul said, "Though I speak with the tongue of men and angels, and have not charity, I am become as sounding brass or a tinkling cymbal."

You could also carry openness to a potentially dangerous extreme by forcing yourself, for instance, to meet and socialize with someone your partner has expressed an interest in. You might get along fantastically. But then again you might not. It will all depend on how you feel about yourself. And there could be a problem even if your rival isn't better looking, brighter or more vibrant than you. Your response might be, "He/she likes *that* better than me?" Depending on your sense of self-worth, you'll feel worse or better after the experience.

Staying in love is like walking a tightrope. To do it successfully the partners must be prepared to perform, in effect, a balancing act between being straightforward and being reserved, between closeness and distance, between responsibility to oneself and responsibility to the other. It is not an easy walk, nor does it become easier as you grow older. Love is not always moonlight and roses and tea-for-two-me-for-you. It takes work and sacrifice, sharing and caring, and sometimes it means loving a little less so that you can love longer. Understand, also, that when you love, jealousy will be there as well.

But even jealousy, painful as it is, has some value. It can warn you that it's time to sit down and talk seriously about your relationship, your needs, how much you're willing to give, how much you're willing to accept. When you do that, when you talk and listen, it can't help benefiting the relationship. Jealousy can force you to look closely at yourself, if you take advantage of it, and you might, once again, learn enough about yourself to make you a better individual. It can, when you admit to feeling jealous, make you less apt to react irrationally when your partner does something to conjure up the green-eyed monster.

Jealousy isn't going to be eliminated from our collection of negative emotions any more than is anger, which it generates. You're going to feel it again and again whenever someone gets in the way of your relationship with another. The important thing is that you recognize it, and try to get behind it so that you can determine why you feel the way you do. If you can do that, you will have accomplished a great deal, and your relationship, if it's built on anything solid, will become stronger.

5

Pornography

IF JEALOUSY CAN HURT and blind us so that we forget
love and all the warmth of feeling it can bring, there is yet another obstruction to love. Although it is not, as jealousy is, an
emotion, it is as common and may be as damaging to relationships between young people. I speak of pornography, the explicit portrayal in books, movies and onstage of various sexual
acts. It's sole purpose is to arouse desire. Whether it be so-called
hard-core or soft-core pornography (the former depicting actual
sex, the latter simulated) the aim is to turn us on sexually.
Glossy "skin magazines" on the racks of virtually every variety
store and pharmacy display men and women in erotic poses;
"skin flicks" are the stock-in-trade of drive-in movies across the
country; topless and bottomless waitresses serve food and drink
in the so-called adult entertainment sections of many large cities;
porno bars featuring nude dancers, male and female, swaying
to flashing lights and pulsing disco music have sprung up. One

such bar in New York City recently made some additions to its array of nude dancers: television sets featuring pornographic movies and, for other tastes, live sex shows on a large bed off to a side of the main room.

One might argue that such presentations have their place, and maybe even some value. Nonetheless, when sexual themes are as dominant as they are in pornography, and are presented, as they often are, in a repulsive, depraved and even violent manner, then sex becomes dehumanized, and love is transformed from a beautiful four-letter word to a common, harsher one. Sex without love is what pornography is all about.

Although there isn't space in a book of this sort to fully analyze the legal tangles that have developed around pornography and obscenity laws over the years, some discussion of the legal issues and the history of obscenity might serve as helpful background to an overall consideration of how an overemphasis on sex can injure a love relationship, or stop one from forming. It should be pointed out here that the term *pornographic* has no legal significance. Some people often use it interchangeably with *erotic,* which means anything that can arouse us sexually. There is, however, some difference of opinion over whether erotic material is necessarily pornographic. Obscenity, on the other hand, is a legal concept under which certain publications can be banned or restricted because of their graphic treatment of sexual material. Definitions of obscenity usually include phrases such as "disgusting to the senses," "abhorrent to morality and virtue," "designed to incite to depravity or lust."

Pornography (or erotic material) does not belong solely to the twentieth century. Admittedly, sexual explicitness has risen (or sunk, depending on your perception of the matter) to new levels in the last few years, due in part to changing attitudes toward sexual behavior and the desire for more personal flexibility in the making of moral decisions. But one can go back to the cave paintings of primitive peoples for examples of what we find today on the walls of public toilets. *Graffiti,* these wall scribblings are called, a name that was originally applied to the pictographs found at Pompeii and other ancient Italian cities. "We might not have guessed the keenness of Pompeii's life had not its people scratched their sentiments upon public walls," writes historian Will Durant. "Three thousand such graffiti have been copied there, and presumably there were thousands more. . . . Sometimes the authors merely inscribed their names or obscene audacities, as men still love to do. . . . Many of the inscriptions are love messages, often in verse: Romula notes that she 'tarried here with Stephylus . . .' "[1] Pompeii's walls and, indeed, those of early Greek and Egyptian cities, venerated the phallus, or penis. Common also were scenes of sexual intercourse, and of Satyrs, woodland deities part man and part goat, pursuing, with penises erect, lovely nymphs.

It should be noted that while many of the erotic scenes depicted in early art were undoubtedly meant to arouse sexual desire, many more were not. Drs. Herant A. Katchadourian and Donald T. Lunde of Stanford University's Department of Psychiatry have this to say about it:

> The great abundance of sexual references in prehistoric and primitive art does not reflect a mood of carefree hedonism in early civilizations, but a concern with urgent human needs and most particularly with the preservation of life itself. Sexual art at this stage was magical art, having very little to do with individual experience or pleasure. Sexual imagery served to explain the mysterious origins of human

life, the motion of the sun and moon, the cycle of the seasons, and man's existence after death. . . . The basic connection between agriculture, with its reliance on fecundity, and the early growth of culture helps to account for the prevalence of sexual content in early art, as well as in early myth, drama and dance.[2]

And so, they point out, we have fields and flocks of rural Greece guarded by phallic pillars or statues, and chiseled into monuments is Priapus, god of animal and vegetable fertility, with an erect penis.

Taken out of context, much of early erotic art could be regarded as pornographic by today's standards. For example, a sixteenth-century Indian temple relief depicting group sexual intercourse for the purpose of venerating pregnancy and birth could be reproduced in a modern-day skin magazine and captioned with an obscene joke. The religious and cultural significance would, obviously, be lost.

What does and does not constitute obscene material? Those are difficult questions, to say the least. Bear two points in mind before going on. The first is an expression that journalists have seen proven time and again. It is, "One person's blizzard is another person's ski trip." Applied to the stories written in newspapers and magazines, this means that someone can like and appreciate an article, and will write glowing letters of praise to the author. Others will hate the very same piece, and will send incredibly nasty notes of criticism to the writer. The other point is one that will recur throughout this book, and that is that sex is not evil or immoral in itself, and neither is the unclad human body. Many people don't agree with that — either out of a deep religious conviction, because they were brought up with certain values, or because some event or person has helped to repress or poorly shape their attitudes toward sexuality. It is not my intent to debate those who hold such views.

Bearing those two points in mind — that one person's blizzard is another's ski trip, and that sex in itself is not wrong — let's look at the question of what constitutes obscene material.

For years, the courts, legislatures, police, private citizens and community organizations have struggled with the obscenity issue. Back in the early 1700s, a Scottish bookseller in London named Alexander Cruden petitioned Parliament to name him "Corrector of the People." Confined to insane asylums several times, he assumed the nickname Alexander the Corrector, and went about town on his moral crusade, wet sponge in hand, wiping away obscenities scrawled on buildings and walls. He was, in a sense, acting as Carrie Nation did. She was the vocal temperance agitator who early in the 1900s was convinced she was divinely chosen to wipe out saloons. Armed with a hatchet, she wrecked a good number of barrooms in Medicine Lodge, Kansas, was jailed often, and was generally ridiculed.

Before the nineteenth century, English common law prohibited the distribution of sexual information, but only when it was part of antireligious or antigovernment publications. Later, in 1857, the first general obscenity statute was passed in England. Among the colonies, only Massachusetts enacted such a statute, and in 1821, Vermont became the first state to legislate against obscenity. In 1842, in a move aimed at stemming the flow into the United States of obscene "French postcards," the first federal statute went on the books. This was followed, two decades later, by a congressional ban on using the mails to disseminate obscene material.

In the latter part of the nineteenth century, through the efforts of an American reformer, Anthony Comstock, obscenity-law enforcement was widespread. In 1873, Comstock helped organize the New York Society for the Suppression of Vice and devoted his energies to crusades against books, pictures and establishments that he considered dangerous to public morals. Credited with convicting some twenty-five hundred persons on morals charges, he was responsible for passage of the so-called Comstock Laws, which were concerned with the aforementioned obscene materials in the U.S. mails. By the end of the nineteenth century some thirty states had general anti-obscenity laws in force, and by the middle of the twentieth century all states had some form of law against obscenity.

But legislating against pornography is one thing, defining it is quite another. As late as 1961, in fact, American dictionaries defined pornography only as the "description or portrayal of prostitutes or prostitution." Later, this was extended to include "obscene or licentious writing, painting or the like," a definition that generally holds today. In Japan, pornography is defined as "that which stirs up or excites sexual desire, spoils the normal sexual modesty of the ordinary human being, or is contrary to good sexual morals." U.S. Supreme Court Justice Potter Stewart put it more simply, however, when he declared that he knew it when he saw it.

That may well be true, but the U.S. Supreme Court still has had a difficult time defining what works may constitutionally be considered obscene. Its efforts in a series of involved cases have not, in fact, always been totally satisfying. One of the chief considerations in deciding what is and is not obscene is, of course, the constitutional guarantee of free speech and press. On the one hand, the high court must reaffirm that right, but on the other it has ruled that the First Amendment protection does not cover obscene material. "Implicit in the history of the First Amendment," the Court ruled in a 1957 case, "is the rejection of obscenity as utterly without redeeming social value." Still, the Court said, just because sex is included in a work does not necessarily mean it is obscene. What must also be considered is whether, to an average individual who applies modern-day community standards, the dominant theme of the material "taken as a whole appeals to the prurient [lewd] interest." Moreover, the Court found, such material must be "patently offensive" and "utterly without redeeming social value." In 1966, the high court handed down another ruling, holding that though a book may not in itself be pornographic, it may be banned because of the way it is advertised and promoted. This prompted the *Chicago Sun-Times* to comment in an editorial:

One wonders what would happen if a frolicsome or unscrupulous promoter should be offensive in the advertising of classics — the Bible, say, or Shakespeare, Cervantes or Dante, all of which have been victims of censorship in the past. Would the works then be subject to censorship? And would a pornographic book be made unpornographic by dignified, restrained, unsuggestive promotion? The thing ought to work both ways. Or consider what Associate Justice William O. Douglas had to say in dissenting: "The advertisements of our best magazines are chock-full of thighs, ankles, calves, bosoms, eyes, and hair, to draw the potential buyers' attention to lotions, tires, food, liquor, clothing, autos and even insurance policies. The sexy advertisement neither adds to nor detracts from the quality of the merchandise. . . . A book should stand on its own, irrespective of the reasons why it was written or the wiles used in selling it."

Whatever the varying opinions upon the Supreme Court's new dictum, everybody can agree that it hasn't heard the last of the problem. The Court has invited a whole new attack upon books, publishers and writers, and so has invited more work for itself. Close decisions often make bad law, and Monday's made bad law indeed."[3]

In 1969, the Court said that under the First Amendment an individual is allowed to have whatever material he or she wants in the home, even if it is obscene. Prosecution for private possession of pornographic material, then, is unjust. There have been several other rulings, some quite incomprehensible to the nonlegal mind, others inconsistent with other cases. In general, as matters stand today, individual states have the right to pass laws banning works that "appeal to the prurient interest in sex, which portray sexual conduct in a patently offensive way, and which, taken as a whole, do not have serious literary, artistic, political or scientific value." Determining what is "prurient" or "patently offensive" is left, under the recent rulings, to local judgment. The difficulty with applying community standards, though, is that it's another case of one person's blizzard being another's ski trip. After a recent anti-obscenity ruling, Episcopal priest Malcolm Boyd, author of the best-selling book *Are You Running with Me, Jesus?*, had this to say: "Movies will suffer irremediably. For what is 'patently offensive' to one person is 'patently inoffensive' to another. 'Prurient' or 'dirty' in one person's view is 'healthy' or 'clean' according to another's standard."[4]

Thus, one community could ban the controversial movie *Deep Throat* or the magazine *Playboy,* but another might not. Carried to a further extreme, some of the Court's rulings could be used to suppress important works, as the newspaper editorial we cited suggested, simply because certain community leaders are personally offended by them. A classic example of this was the U.S. government's attempt many years ago to block the importing of James Joyce's great novel, *Ulysses*. In 1933, however, the U.S. District Court in New York ruled that it was not obscene. Similarly, a number of communities objected to J. D. Salinger's novel *Catcher in the Rye* being used in high schools, and several others have taken a dim view of sex education books. In many cases the principal objection — and it usually comes from overzealous school administrators, school committees or PTA members — has been to "dirty" words or "foul" language. Undoubtedly, most people have heard or used language that is not considered proper by many people. But, as vulgar and crude and offensive as such language may be, the mere use of it does not make any work in which it appears — movie, book or play — obscene. Such words might well appear in works that are pornographic, but in themselves they are not.

A case in point is the Supreme Court's recent ruling that the Federal Communications Commission (FCC) may warn a radio or television broadcaster that the station may be penalized for airing offensive words. Comedian George Carlin — whose recording of a monologue called "Filthy Words" brought on the Court's ruling — had this to say about it: "People can be immoral, and they can use the words immorally, but I don't think the words themselves are. The philosophical issue — which, of course, doesn't come into play at all [in the Court's decision] — is, are these words worth hiding from? Do they have a power over us? The answer seems to be yes." Carlin made another valid point when he added that "some of the things politicians say qualify as indecent, and I think some of the things big industries say to me on radio and television are indecent." The Authors' League, also, came out on the side of free expression, saying that banning such words would prevent stations from broadcasting readings from books, essays and poetry by many eminent writers — works that employ these words in depictions of sex that are not obscene, or use words in nonsexual contexts, or use them to denote many of their nonsexual meanings. Moreover, the league argued, the FCC's contention that the ban was needed to protect children was invalid for the reason that the seven dirty words in question are in common usage in the street.

Censorship in any form, especially in a democratic society such as our own, is an extremely dangerous policy. Abridgment of the constitutional right of free speech and press paves the way toward an authoritarian state where only the views and values of the current leadership will prevail. Wrote U.S. Supreme Court Justice Potter Stewart in a 1966 case: "Censorship reflects society's lack of confidence in itself. It is a hallmark of an authoritarian regime. . . . So it is that the Constitution protects coarse expression as well as refined, and vulgarity no less than elegance."

We should all be wary of hard-line moralists, antismut vigilantes and other individuals of limited vision who, because they see perversions in every bed, seek to ban works of very real worth. And let's not forget that "an obscenity" is a term that may be applied to anything offensive and disgusting, and should not be restricted to sexual matters. Again, Malcolm Boyd: "Ours is a society that does tragic things, obscene things, in the contexts of power, greed, racism and war. Yet it is the physical relations between human beings, the sexual relations, that we term obscene."[5] A recent case in Georgia illustrates this. J. B. Stoner, a candidate for governor, said in a political radio advertisement, "If Governor George Busbee is reelected, he will pass more civil rights that take from the whites and give to the niggers." Julian Bond, representing the Atlanta chapter of the NAACP, informed the FCC that if Stoner was not prohibited from using the word *nigger* on the air, he would buy air time and have someone recite the "dirty words" the Court ruled were offensive.

Freedom of speech, however, carries responsibility with it. It is difficult to condone someone's falsely crying "Fire!" in a crowded movie theater; disclosing military secrets when the country's survival depends on them; lying in court, in articles or in advertisements; or maliciously hassling someone by mail, telephone or in a newspaper. There is also that quality known as "taste," which we all ought to develop, a style and a form that respects the general rule of propriety and does not cheapen. The use of "dirty" words, obscene gestures and pornographic material should not be encouraged. But it is true that individual opinions of right and wrong, decency and perversion, differ markedly. In 1973, after one of the Supreme Court rulings on obscenity, store owners in Boise, Idaho, immediately removed all "skin" magazines from their racks, including one of the oldest and most popular, *Playboy.* The state's attorney general, who was an innovator of a state law that banned all "obviously obscene" publications, commented that he was befuddled by the move and that he liked to read the magazine once in a while. Storekeepers, he suggested, were being overcautious until the law could determine just which magazines were legal and which were not.

In addition, we can generally choose whether or not to use vulgar language, attend obscene performances, or read erotic material. In an article titled "Porno Chic" in *Playboy,* a magazine that has come in for its share of criticism over the years, writer Bruce Williamson makes it clear that at its worst, pornography is "dreary, tasteless, anti-erotic, expensive and excruciatingly dull — but seldom, if ever, compulsory." Hard-core sex for consenting adults, he adds, has been called a crime, "but no one has yet been able to identify its victims."

A few years ago, an experiment was conducted at the University of North Carolina. Young men over age twenty-one were continually shown pornographic films, pictures and books. The scientists conducting the study found that this constant exposure usually led to boredom rather than sexual arousal. A similar experiment with middle-aged couples in Palo Alto, California, indicated that pornography excited the couples to more than normal sexual activity, but that the effects did not last long. A member of another pornography study commented, "We have four file drawers full of the stuff and everybody is so tired of it that we can't get anybody to look at it anymore."

While a constant exposure to pornography would probably turn more people off than on, it has been argued that occasional encounters with erotic material have some merit. It stimulates fantasy, say the psychologists, and this can be good either as a pleasant diversion or as a way to exercise the mind. Sexual fantasy is a normal activity and one should not feel guilty or depraved for having engaged in such a pastime. It becomes a problem only when it takes up so much of our time and energy — or tends to become so perverse or violent — that it interferes with the ability to maintain normal relationships or fulfill responsibilities.

Many psychologists have also suggested that the earlier people are exposed to erotic material, the less apt they are to develop sexual problems later on in life. If one had to make a choice between being raised in a sexual vacuum where the subject of sex is never discussed (or where, if it is, it's painted with a heavy brushload of sin), or being raised in an atmosphere of honesty about sex, even with exposure to erotica, it would be far better to choose the latter. Repressed and poorly shaped attitudes toward sexuality have been behind too many sexual deviations and maladjustments for us to err on the side of silence or dishonesty and failure to accept the fact that we are sexual beings.

Pornography has also played a part in sex education courses and in some medical schools and colleges, as well as in the work of those who deal with couples whose sex lives are not satisfactory. A few years ago, a class that made use of pornographic films was conducted at the Johns Hopkins School of Medicine. It was called a "direct-confrontation" sex education course. According to Dr. John W. Money, who taught it, the course was designed to encourage students to reexamine their attitudes toward sexual customs and to develop enough objectivity to help them deal with patients' sexual problems. Also, students who took the course were expected to come to a clearer understanding of their own sexuality and moral values, and it was hoped they might become part of a new generation of medical students "who could go out as consultants in their communities, able to conduct discussion groups and give expert testimony when it is needed."[6] Physicians, we ought to point out here, are just as lacking in understanding of human sexuality as most everybody else is. Although their training in anatomy and physiology has taught them a great deal about the sexual organs, they rarely learn much in school about sexual activities or about the psychological aspects of sexuality. The use of audiovisual materials that focus on sexually explicit themes thus might be one way to help them give better care to patients who come to them for sexual counseling.

In a similar vein, Fairleigh Dickinson University recently conducted a "sexual attitude reassessment workshop" for undergraduate students. Hard-core pornographic and explicit sex education films were screened in a school auditorium hung with pinup photographs from sex magazines. The film program, a required portion of a biology course in human sexuality that dealt with venereal disease, pregnancy and birth control, was followed by group discussion. Dr. Robert T. Francoeur, who was in charge of the program, saw its approach as a means of easing some of the embarrassment students might feel over sexual matters, making it easier for them to have a loving relationship.

The format of the film portion of the program bears special mention because of the way in which it depicted sex. One segment of the film program showed sleazy X-rated movies with titles like *Door to Door Sex* and *Western Orgy*. Another portion screened a film made by college students, showing nude men and women romping about but not engaging in any sexual activity. Still another featured legitimate sex education films showing sexual intercourse in peaceful settings, on the beach and in a field. The mix of films was intended to demonstrate how sex — again, not in itself "dirty" — can be presented with tenderness and as an expression of love, or as a debasing experience that is especially inconsiderate of women.

It's unlikely that pornography, hard core or soft, is going to trigger instant debauchery, or enough sexual immorality to transform the civilized world into a modern Sodom and Gomorrah to be destroyed by a vengeful God. It will not make all men rapists and all women seductresses. Obscenity is, rather, a human reality, a human frailty, if you will, that is better faced than denied, a fact of life that is more nuisance than evil. A number of studies have shown, however, that when we are exposed to erotic material, we tend to talk more about sex. Sometimes, this exposure leads us to try things we wouldn't ordinarily try, and, some psychologists suggest, makes us more apt to agree that it's okay to have sex without affection. Other studies have dealt with the question of whether exposure to pornography causes aggressive behavior.

A special presidential commission in 1970 was unable to turn up any evidence that sex crimes are linked to pornography, but some recent investigations suggest that erotic material may very well heighten male aggression toward women, especially in men who are inclined toward such behavior. One such study was conducted at Iowa State University of Science and Technology. A group of students was asked to write essays on such topics as Richard Nixon's presidency, and removal of criminal penalties for possession of marijuana. The essays were criticized by other students who not only evaluated them but added insults or compliments. Then, the students who wrote the essays were encouraged to get back at the reviewers by giving them an electrical shock with a special laboratory machine. First, some of the essay writers were shown erotic or aggressive films, and some were not. Three findings emerged from the study. One was that students who watched the pornographic films were very aggressive in administering shocks to critical reviewers. The second was that those who had been made angry by the reviews but not exposed to the films were not as aggressive. And the third finding was that the men were more aggressive toward women than women were toward men, an interesting conclusion.

The very real dangers in pornography have to do with how it neglects love, and how it portrays women as nameless objects of passion in which men can relieve themselves. Sealed off from love and consideration and esteem, as men are by pornography, it is no wonder that the stunning, always-available beauties of the hard-core-porn world blind a young man to the realities of a woman's sex. It can affect women as well.

We are all aware that young women are usually brought up to try and make themselves as attractive as possible. There is nothing wrong with this, no more than it is wrong for a young man to be raised with the idea that his appearance is important. But it becomes a problem when beauty is the major concern. A young woman, particularly, is either taught by parents or conditioned by cosmetic advertisements to believe that if she is to have any worth as a woman, if she is to be popular with men, she must be beautiful, and sexy.

Again, there is nothing especially wrong with a woman being beautiful and sexy. But the overemphasis on sex that is found in pornographic material contributes to misunderstanding, to a misplaced system of values.

I recall listening several years ago, when I was on an assignment for my newspaper to the South Pole, to a group of men discuss how they responded to women after spending a year in all-male isolation at the bottom of the world. At the pole station, as at many others on the continent of Antarctica (and in men's prisons, too), the walls of the huts and barracks are literally papered with pinups and centerfolds from every variety of sex magazine — women, nude and perfectly built, all beautiful and sensuous and posed provocatively. An occasional encounter with such material, of course, does no harm. But a steady assault on the senses to the exclusion of all else does give a young man a rather unreal view of females. "It sounds ridiculous, I know, but when I left the ice and got back to civilization," one graduate student told me, "the thing that struck me most was that all the women I passed on the street had clothes on. And they didn't really look all that great to me. I noticed a lot of bad complexions. They also didn't pay much attention to me, which isn't what I was expecting at all. The other thing was their voices, high-pitched and sing-songy, and that sort of grated on my nerves. I also wasn't sure that I'd be able to carry on a conversation with a girl, so you know what the first thing I did was? I headed straight for a topless bar and just sat around watching the waitresses and the dancers."

What is the relationship of women to pornography? Caryl Rivers, an author and associate professor of journalism at Boston University, has characterized pornography as being to women what Nazi propaganda was to Jews. "Pornography portrays women as evil, subhuman and grotesque creatures and creates a climate where it is all right to maim, rape and murder them," she says. One of the goals of Nazi anti-Jewish campaigns, she adds, was to portray Jews as legal prey, thus making violence against them acceptable. "They were shown as evil, as female sexuality is portrayed by pornography, as ugly, and as holders of inordinate economic power. In the same way, pornography makes women fair game." Rivers feels strongly that a journalist's First Amendment rights must be protected. But she readily acknowledges that she found herself cheering for "the other side" when *Hustler* magazine publisher Larry Flynt was arrested. In a recent address before the New England Women's Press Association, Rivers criticized a *New York Times* advertisement on Flynt's behalf, signed by American literary figures. In the advertisement, the publisher was compared with dissident

Soviet artists and writers. "Whatever Flynt is," said Rivers, "he's no Solzhenitsyn." The advertisement, she said, was a clue to how the liberal establishment deals with every issue in pornography — by assuming it is only about freedom of the press and nothing else. "That casts the pornography debate as one of righteous, wonderful First Amendment folk against fundamentalists, who want to hunt down and burn every copy of *Catcher in the Rye*."

A woman who attended a national conference on feminist perspectives on pornography in San Francisco in 1978 put it this way: "Women are dismembered by pornography. Dehumanized. That's the first step to violence. Once we're seen as objects it makes it easier to hurt us. . . . Pornography has a male point of view. Women are just props. If anything should be held basic and human to us, it should be love and sex. Look at those images on Broadway. The neon signs. They're hateful. They're crass and cruel. My daughter refuses to step on Broadway. It frightens her to see images of women's bodies like that. I try to tell her Broadway used to be a beautiful street, full of music, jazz and love. Now we're sickened by the images." Then she told the reporter who had been interviewing her, "It's hard for you to understand, you were brought up as a man in this culture."[7]

Women themselves respond to pornography in different ways. Obviously the ones who make a living from pornography don't object to it. They feel they're giving men what they want and some refer to women who oppose sexually explicit material as man-haters or lesbians. Others make a distinction between pornography and erotica, saying the latter emphasizes sex, but with beauty and feeling. Pornography, they argue, is simply raw sex.

It would be nice if, in one clean sweep, we could cut away the appetite for pornography. But that is not going to happen, and there will always be people among us — mostly men — who will delight in it and who will be affected by it and who will never see what it does to them and to the way they relate to others. That is the nature of things. But we can learn to recognize where erotica — which can be acceptable, pleasurable and noninjurious to your emotional health — changes from something that arouses sexual love to something that debases the beauty and the mystery of the act of sex.

We can learn to tell the difference between erotica and pornography by asking questions that have been implied thus far. Do the nude pictures, the sexual contortions they illustrate, make woman a slave to man? Do they tend to degrade her? There's an X-rated movie in town. How would you feel about taking the straightest student in your class to see it? If your answer is "No way," why? If you would, why? Look at some erotica and rate it. Which of it would you classify as obscene? Why? If it is obscene, should it be banned? If your answer is yes, what would be some of the repercussions of such an action?

These are important questions, and although your answers won't do much to change the current state of affairs, they will help you figure out where pornography fits in the sexual scenario. They might also help you to make the right choice when you have to translate your encounter with erotic material to an encounter with a real partner.

6

Prostitution

In the discussion of homosexuality it was said that even though it is not regarded as "normal" behavior in our predominantly heterosexual culture, it nevertheless involves entirely normal emotions: caring, liking, loving. But this is not the case with the activity that is as old as civilization itself, prostitution.

Prostitutes — most are women, but some homosexual males pursue the "occupation" — offer sex for a price. They might work on their own, for someone called a pimp (a panderer who takes a share of their earnings), or in a "house." Rarely, if ever, does emotional attachment or affection enter into a relationship between a prostitute and clients, and when a prostitute asks a customer, "Can I do something for you?" the approach should not be confused with that of lovers who are considerate of each other's needs. The prostitute has no personal interest whatsoever in her customer, and couldn't care less about him once the acts of sexual intimacy are done. She is simply selling a service, just as the dry cleaner on the corner sells its service.

There are different names for a prostitute. Some are rather old-fashioned and pleasant-sounding, and they almost soften the hardness of the profession — courtesan, cocotte, *fille de joie* and meretrix. Others have a street harshness about them — whore, hooker, slut, call girl, lady of the night, glitter princess, tart, strumpet and trollop. There are also names for the prostitutes' clients; the most common is "john." When a prostitute "turns a trick," she has sex with a customer. Equally imaginative are the synonyms for houses of prostitution — bordello, brothel, house of ill fame, house of ill repute, whorehouse, bawdy house, cathouse. A place where there are many houses of prostitution or prostitutes is called a "red-light district," or "the tenderloin."

Prostitution, as has been stated, was known in the earliest times. Kublai Khan, first emperor of the Mongol dynasty in China, provided prostitutes free of charge to the many foreign adventurers who visited his stately courts. Marco Polo, the famous Venetian traveler, who spent much time with the Khan, reported that they were women of incredible beauty. In China, it was regarded as perfectly normal for a young man to visit prostitutes on occasion, as it was in Greece and Rome, where those who were visited were taxed. In some early societies, prostitution was part of a religious rite, and so-called temple prostitutes had intercourse with visitors as an offering to one goddess or another. The Greek historian Herodotus tells us that the Babylonians were among those who combined prostitution with religion. "Every native woman," he writes, "is obliged once in her life to sit in the Temple of Venus, and have intercourse with some stranger. . . . When a woman has once seated herself, she must not return home until some stranger has thrown a piece of silver in her lap, and lain with her outside the temple. . . . The woman follows the first man that throws, and refuses no one."[1] Unlike the conventional prostitute of today, however, the temple prostitute was forbidden to engage in intercourse for money once her period of duty in the temple was over.

In America, prostitution dates back to colonial times, and it was not only soldiers, merchant seamen and those who hung out in wayside and wharfside taverns who patronized the bawdy houses. Just as today, some of the country's most prominent leaders, married as well as single, hired women "of easy virtue" for sex.

It is interesting that prostitution generally flourishes in societies where there is limited sexual freedom. Cultures such as those of North American Indians and natives of New Guinea, for example, know about sex and engage in various sexual activities at an early age. These groups have found no need to purchase sex. The males in some of these societies, it is true, may present gifts, in the form of food or jewelry, to the women from whom they ask sexual favors, but this behavior is not considered a form of prostitution. Instead, say anthropologists who have studied such practices, it closely resembles the familiar practice in our society of a lover's bringing flowers or candy to his girl. Real prostitution, again, thrives in societies that have taken a stern stand on sex — either through laws forbidding certain practices or through moral codes that favor marriage and family. Virtually all human societies, even those with a more permissive attitude toward sex, have some sort of rules governing sexual behavior, and few, if any, actually condone promiscuity.

But, as widespread as prostitution is, it accounts for a relatively small proportion of all the sexual activity that goes on during any given day anywhere. And although it probably will always be with us, there are indications that the numbers of young men seeking out prostitutes because they are the only sexual partners available are dwindling. Part of this shift has to do, of course, with the more relaxed attitudes toward sex. But part of it, too, I like to believe, may have something to do with how more and more men are perceiving women — not as sex objects to whom they are emotionally indifferent, but as members of the opposite sex toward whom they can direct genuine affection. (It has been argued that the opposite is true, that many young men are turning to prostitutes because the women's movement, with its emphasis on sexual equality, has upset the traditional role of the male as pursuer.)

But although prostitution is far from being an epidemic of moral degradation, it is still a matter of concern. Many people believe prostitution is morally wrong, just as they believe sex between unmarried persons, adultery, homosexuality, pornography and drinking are morally wrong. For those who are opposed to it on this ground, prostitution runs counter to the laws of God. "Whoremongers, and adulterers, God will judge," warns the Bible in one oft-quoted passage. "A whore is a deep ditch," it says in another.

Others, physicians and sociologists among them, feel that prostitution is both a public health problem and a sign of a community's social disorganization. They point out that prostitutes who work the streets are responsible for the spread of venereal disease, and that often they are not so much interested in providing "fun" for a customer as they are in robbing him. Stories of patrons being assaulted, even murdered, by prostitutes or pimps are not uncommon, and they are often true. Moreover, prostitution, which has traditionally been an urban blight — as well as a fixture wherever men are away from women, be it on the Alaska pipeline or a desert army post — has begun to spread to suburban hotels, motels and apartment complexes.

As prostitution spreads, it carries not only the likelihood of street crime and venereal disease — the last a major problem where there is any promiscuous sexual activity, be it prostitution or indiscriminate sex with many partners — but also the possible involvement of organized crime. Just as big-city racketeers were involved in the lucrative illegal liquor trade during Prohibition days and are involved nowadays in supplying drugs, so, too, are they often behind prostitution rings. Another unpleasant spin-off from prostitution is that many young prostitutes are also drug addicts, a habit they have acquired to mask the guilt and the low self-esteem they often have because of their way of life and because of the distasteful way society views them. Some of these women were prostitutes before they became drug addicts. Others were addicts first. In whatever category they fit, however, the fact is that prostitution, and sometimes robbery, is how they get the money to support the habit.

There are many laws forbidding prostitution. Most of them make it a crime for someone to *be* a prostitute and few punish her customers. This means that the prostitute is usually arrested and charged with what is formally known as soliciting — that is, enticing someone to participate in an immoral or illegal act. The man generally goes free. Every so often, though, one reads of an arrest that takes in both prostitute as solicitor and customer as accomplice in breaking the law. Recently in Des Moines, Iowa, nine men, including a university president and an assistant state attorney general, were arrested for trying to buy sex from a woman police officer who posed as a prostitute. This time, the men were charged with soliciting for prostitution and faced a sentence of up to two years in jail and a five-thousand-dollar fine. Many people, including members of women's organizations, feel that failure to punish the customer is misplaced justice. They argue that if there were no customers there would be no prostitution, and that the man is as guilty of breaking the law as the woman is. The situation, they contend, is one more example of the double standard that is applied to the activities of men and women, a sore reminder of the upper hand that men have always had in matters of sex.

Another example of a dual standard is the fact that most police crackdowns on prostitutes tend to concentrate on street-walking women who work sleazy downtown areas and who are more visible and thus more offensive. Most of these women charge relatively little for their services and, as we said earlier, have often turned to prostitution to support a drug habit. On the other hand, the more sophisticated-appearing call girls, well-groomed and lovely young women who charge one hundred dollars a night and more and whose clients include prominent citizens, usually manage to stay out of trouble with the law. While it is not true in every case, one cannot overlook the fact that too often, the more influence and money one has, the easier it is to get away with everything from murder to white-collar crime. And while most policemen and other law-enforcement officials do their jobs as they are supposed to, there are a few who will look the other way when a notable figure is involved in a vice raid, and who might even accept bribes, in the form of money or a prostitute's services, to allow prostitution to continue.

One of the strongest laws aimed at stifling prostitution is known as the Mann Act. Also called the White Slave Act, this law, passed by Congress in 1910, forbade transporting a woman from one state to another for prostitution "or for any other immoral purpose," an activity engaged in by many Prohibition-era gangsters. Unfortunately, as often happens when any law is sternly adhered to or broadly interpreted, innocent individuals are caught up in its sweep. A number of men have been arrested under the Mann Act for traveling over state borders with women companions and then having sex with them. Sometimes the men have been the victims of vindictive women who want to punish the men for some insult or injury and talk them into crossing a state line. Other times, they are the victims of law-enforcement officials looking for an excuse.

Ten years after the Mann Act was passed, the Committee on Traffic in Women and Children of the League of Nations was formed. This was followed, twenty years later, by the May Act. The act was prompted both by widespread prostitution and venereal disease and by America's entrance into World War II. Physicians who were examining young men for induction into the armed services found that one out of fifty had syphilis, the most dangerous of the major venereal diseases. The May Act, which prohibited prostitution near military bases, laid the groundwork for federal control of prostitution and did much to cut the VD rate.

Some countries, however, tolerate prostitution, even though they may have no laws that officially condone it. In the United

States, in fact, houses of prostitution have been allowed in some rural counties in Nevada, although the activity is outlawed in Las Vegas and Reno. Nonetheless, as any tourist to the two gambling centers will confirm, prostitutes operate relatively openly in the lobbies and bars of many hotels, just as they do in every major city in the country.

The argument over whether to suppress prostitution by enforcing the laws more strongly, or to allow it to operate under certain regulations, is a long-standing one. Those who believe that prostitution can be regulated feel that, as in the unsuccessful attempt to ban liquor during Prohibition years, banning prostitution would be as effective as passing a law prohibiting hatred. Many men, it is argued, will always demand the services of a prostitute for a wide variety of reasons — satisfaction with no legal or emotional obligations, curiosity, variety or simply their inability to attract women. In a number of countries, in fact, a high proportion of premarital sex has traditionally been obtained from prostitutes by men who, because of the strict culture they have been brought up in, value virginity in other women, particularly the ones they hope to marry. We are all familiar with the Spanish duenna, the female guardian who accompanies young women of socially respectable families. This kind of tradition has undoubtedly strengthened the males' attitude that "nice" women don't have sex freely, and allows them to become better acquainted with prostitutes, who do. According to the Kinsey studies of sexual behavior, so strict is the tradition against premarital sex for girls of "better" families that some Spanish and European males find it difficult to have sex with their wives because they hold the same respect for them that they hold for their mothers, sisters and all "decent" women.

Consequently, some men may continue to have sex with prostitutes even after they marry, or they may seek out mistresses, thus preserving their wives' "goodness."[2]

Some people have argued that legalizing prostitution would offer an outlet for men whose pent-up passions might cause them to commit sex crimes. Others say that if prostitution were approved, regulations would be included to provide for periodic medical examinations that would lessen, not increase, the incidence of venereal disease. The latter argument has some strength in light of a recent report that although Nevada has the third highest VD rate in the country, the houses of prostitution contribute very little to the problem. Most women who work in the legal brothels are conscious of their health and, according to medical specialists, much of the VD in the state is attributable to unsupervised streetwalkers and to casual sex among strangers.

Some of the reasons given for legalizing prostitution may have some merit. Moreover, any man would probably sound quite self-righteous if he stated unequivocally that, even if he were working for a long period of time in a remote area and prostitutes were the only means of obtaining sexual satisfaction, he would never visit one. Circumstances govern many of the choices we make, and both the spirit and the flesh are, indeed, weak on occasion.

Most people, however, would probably agree that prostitution causes more trouble than it prevents. The "happy hooker," with her favorite customers in a house of fun, and the dutiful daughter, who's only doing it to help support her widowed mother, are but characters in movies or novels. The prostitute's real world is one that is devoid of affection and respect, one in which suicide is often the only choice she feels she has when life gets tougher than she can bear. It is a grim world of beatings and other forms of physical abuse, of jail cells and junkies, perverts and pimps whose view of sex has not progressed above the belt buckle. One soon forgets the fun and games and the sexy shady ladies of the films when confronted with a heart-wrenching incident like the one that occurred recently in Vermont.

It involved an eighteen-year-old girl named Judy who went to Boston to enter college. In a short time, she became involved with a pimp and began working for him as a prostitute. Her mother found out and managed to bring her back home, and tried to convince her to remain. The pimp began to telephone, and Judy decided to return to him. Distraught and frustrated, her mother took two of her husband's hand guns from a closet, and asked her daughter to go for a ride. There was but one thought in her mind at the time, she said later: "Today is the day she dies." In the parking lot of a synagogue, the mother asked her daughter to get out of the car. "Judy, I can't let you go," she said, as she began shooting. Judy died and her mother was charged with her murder. At her trial, the state's attorney told the court he didn't believe justice would be served by sending the woman to prison for the rest of her life. "It was almost a mercy type of killing," he said.[3]

It might be argued, of course, that no one has the right to kill to stop an individual from choosing an unconventional and, in the mind of some, immoral life-style. The incident, however, does remind us that prostitution is not a particularly savory business.

And what of the women who enter prostitution? Why do they do it? There are many theories. Some suggest that poverty and the desire for luxuries or the need for money to support a drug habit are what make a woman choose this way of life. "I started when I was thirteen," recalls one former prostitute. "I got arrested while I was having sex in the back of a cab with the driver. My dad was a drunk, my mother committed suicide when I was eleven, and my life at home stunk. I needed to feel like I was somebody, and I wanted to look good, even though that was hard because all the money I was making was going into drugs." Others can point to cases where young women have been forced into becoming prostitutes by a pimp's physical threats. But while economic reasons and coercion might play a role at times, the view most accepted today is that psychological reasons are behind a woman's decision to become a prostitute.

It has been suggested, for one thing, that the prostitute hates her father because of his lack of affection, and that she transfers this hatred to her customers by forcing them, in a sense, to become immoral. Thus, she revenges herself against her father by making a man, who represents him, lose his sense of dignity.

"My father was one of those distant and proper kind of guys," says one prostitute, "who rarely paid any attention to my sister and me. Once in a while, when he was off on a trip, he'd buy us stuff, a camera or a watch, a gadget, but he wouldn't say much about the trip, even to mom. Someone called him a father of joy once, and I never knew what that meant till I took this psych course and found it meant a dad who did surfacy things for kids but never talked to them or held them. One time, when he was having a few friends over, I went to the piano and started playing a piece I had just learned, and I wanted them all to hear how good I was at it. Well, my dad just yelled at me to quit it, and he told me, "Look, I'm trying to talk to these people so go do something constructive.' I think about that remark every so often when I'm in bed with some guy, 'Go do something constructive.' "

Some studies suggest that prostitutes are often lesbians, and that they, too, are punishing men by holding the power of sex over them. Not all prostitutes or all lesbians, for that matter, are man-haters, however, and since psychology is such an inexact science, it would be unfair to use man-hating as an argument to explain every prostitute's behavior. Some prostitutes may be women who constantly need to be reminded that they are attractive to men and who delight in being wanted enough for a man to pay them. Others may be oversexed, and prostitution affords them a ready and varied outlet. Still others may regard sex so lightly that it becomes merely another way of making a living.

"It was a tremendous kick," one call girl said of her first trick. "Here I was doing absolutely nothing, and in twenty minutes I was going to walk out with fifty dollars in my pocket. That just made me feel absolutely marvelous. I came downtown. I can't believe this! I'm not changed, I'm the same as I was twenty minutes ago, except that now I have fifty dollars in my pocket. It really was tremendous status. How many people could make fifty dollars for twenty minutes' work? Folks work for eighty dollars take-home pay. I worked twenty minutes for fifty dollars clear, no taxes, nothing. I was still in school, I was smoking grass, I was shooting heroin, I wasn't hooked yet, and I had money. It was terrific."[4]

But no matter what causes it, there should be little doubt in anyone's mind that prostitution hurts women, misrepresents the place of sex in society, and stands in the way of love. It hurts the prostitute herself by making her an object in which a man lets out his lust, and it hurts women in general by reinforcing the male's image of the female as a machine for sex or babies, to be turned on at his whim. Susan Brownmiller, in her widely acclaimed book on rape, *Against Our Will,* alludes to this:

> The myth of the heroic rapist that permeates false notions of masculinity, from the successful seducer to the man who "takes what he wants when he wants it," is inculcated in young boys from the time they first become aware that being a male means access to certain mysterious rites and privileges, including the right to buy a woman's body. When young men learn that females may be bought for a price, and that acts of sex command set prices, then how should they not also conclude that that which may be bought may also be taken without the civility of a monetary exchange? . . . Operating from the old (and discredited) lust, drive and relief theory, men have occasionally put forward the notion that the way to control criminal rape is to ensure the ready accessibility of female bodies at a reasonable price through the legalization of prostitution, so that the male impulse might be satisfied with ease, efficiency and a minimum of bother.[5]

If Kinsey was correct in his estimates, about 70 percent of the total white male population in 1953 had had some experience with prostitutes. The figure, as we suggested earlier, may be lower today. In any event, a good portion of the American male population, and of the male populations of many other countries, is aware that there are women willing to make them happy for a price. It's not too difficult to twist that knowledge into the notion that, as one popular and vulgar expression put it some years ago, "You buy them a little dinner and they'll feed you what you want later," or to believe that there are plenty of women around who will become mistress to a married man in return for a rent-paid penthouse, chic clothes and frequent meals in the best restaurants. You've probably even heard people say, "She married him for his money," in a tone that implies she's giving him sex for it.

Prostitution injures the ideals of romantic love, marriage and family. As one young prostitute put it, "You have to do so much faking when you're having sex with a customer, that's part of the game, making him think he's really getting you exclusively. You do that so often that it becomes difficult to really feel for someone because you're into this big scam, this con game that revolves around sex. So you get pretty hard about it. I don't know if I could ever get married, though some of my friends who do what I do have. First, I think I'm sexually numb anyway, and second I don't know if I'd trust a guy who tells me he really likes me."

If, as a young man, you keep frequent company with prostitutes, you won't be giving real love and affection a chance to grow. Sex becomes but an end in itself, a selfish act for your own pleasure, a momentary leap of the nervous system that is not much better, in truth, than masturbation. The women you will have, attractive though they may be, will be without personality — at least none that you will be allowed to discover — and their last names, the true marks of their identity, will be a mystery to you.

It is very difficult to understand the true meaning of such words as *love* and *like* under such circumstances, for what you are interested in will only be skin deep. Worse, this pale imitation of affection was not offered out of any interest in you. You bought and paid for it, just as your buddy, who might be less appealing than you, could. You've *made* someone love you — and that's not the same as *having* someone love you. The result might well be shallow relationships with other young women you'll meet, a series of affairs that will be trivial because you have not thought much about women as people, only as partners in sexually exploitive situations.

7

Marriage/Living Together

THE BASIC STORY went something like this: A boy and a girl meet and fall in love. They spend most of their time together, usually without other friends along, getting to know one another better. Soon, they marry, go on a honeymoon, and move into an apartment. Later, they buy a home. The husband goes to work every morning and comes home every evening, the wife tends to the children and the household duties. They live happily ever after.

It still works just that way — sometimes.

More often than not today there are variations on this theme of love and marriage. The romantic part of the scenario hasn't changed. Boy and girl still meet, date, and fall in love. But young people have options today that their parents generally did not have. For one thing, when the time comes, they can move into an apartment with a mate without getting married. While many parents still disapprove of such behavior, there are others who hardly take notice of the unmarried couple who live in what used to be called sin. Another option is that the husband may stay home and do the chores while the wife works full time, not merely part time in a department store to make a few extra dollars for Christmas or to help the budget, but in a career that is every bit as much her right to pursue as it is her husband's. There may not even be any children, ever, in the picture anymore. More and more couples are postponing having a family until they feel the time is right. Some have made up their minds that children won't fit into their plans at all. Finally, for those who cannot live happily ever after, there's divorce, with or without remarriage. Divorce has long been an option, of course, but it is more frequent and acceptable nowadays. More than one-half of all teenage marriages have, in fact, ended in divorce.

Even if relatively few of you are planning to get married immediately, you have probably discussed the possibility — even if you've vowed that you will never do such a thing. Most teenagers will marry one day, however, and most will have what is known as a traditional wedding — complete with minister or rabbi or priest, best man and maid of honor, wedding cake and veil and wine and reception and honeymoon. It's important to take a closer look at this serious relationship that is the cornerstone of the family, this social institution that unites one man and one woman to the exclusion of others, and at some of today's marriage options.

Marriages aren't always the natural result of falling in love. People marry for other reasons, even in the United States, where romance generally precedes a wedding. A family might arrange a marriage for business or financial reasons, a king might marry a queen from another country to form a political unit and to solidify power, a young woman from a foreign country might take an American husband to avoid deportation. An old Czech expression leaves little doubt about the weak role Cupid sometimes plays: "Choose your wife not at a dance, but in a harvest field." Some people, because of their own or their culture's taboos about engaging in premarital sexual intercourse, marry so that they may be free to enjoy sex. Others who believe in "doing the right thing" marry because the young woman in the relationship has become pregnant; marriage in a case like this is a way of averting social disgrace.

Whatever the reason for it, marriage usually involves mutual dependence, the founding and raising of a family and, at least in our culture, fidelity, the intention to stay together for life. For though some tribes still sanction "wife-lending" as a form of hospitality to visitors, adultery — which is generally defined as sexual intercourse between two persons who are married but not to each other — is widely frowned upon, prohibited by secular and religious law. We know, of course, that adultery is not uncommon, and that there may be valid reasons why husbands and wives seek the attentions of others. But for the most part, marriage is one man for one woman, or *monogamy.* There is also *bigamy,* which involves marrying another while still legally married, and *polygamy,* a catchall term that includes *polygyny,* in which one man has several wives, and *polyandry,* one woman having several husbands. Polygyny, the most common of these multiple marriages, is still practiced among primitive peoples and was, in fact, acceptable in European Christianity as late as the seventeenth century. A Moslem is allowed to take up to four wives as long as he can support them, but adultery was decreed punishable by death by Mohammed, the prophet who introduced the Moslem faith, Islam. The Mormon

Church, which once condoned plural marriage, outlawed the teaching in 1890 after pressure from Congress.

Getting married in the United States is relatively easy to do despite the enormous responsibilities and emotional involvement it entails. More attention is paid, it sometimes seems, to applicants for automobile drivers' licenses (driver education, a written examination and a road test) than to those who apply to be married. Those who wish to marry need only have reached the legal age of consent, generally eighteen for males and sixteen for females, and their consent must be voluntary. A medical examination is required to screen against the spread of syphilis, and neither of the partners may be married to others at the time of the marriage, nor may the partners be close relatives. The marriage, finally, must be certified by a religious or public official. Each religion has its own requirements or prohibitions, but in the last analysis people are morally and legally free to marry in any church they wish or in a civil ceremony.

Too many individuals take advantage of this ease of entry and, unfortunately, leap into marriage before they look at the true implications of vowing to be together through sickness and health for many years. Hypnotized by music, mate and magic moment, or deluded into believing that marriage will make a drab life exciting, they blurt out, "I do," with little thought to the day when romance fades, as it must, when the honeymoon, in truth, is over. It is not too crass to suggest that the excitement and the newness of *romantic* love wear off in a short time, just as does the novelty of a new outfit or a popular song. It is our biologic nature to lose interest when certain needs are satisfied, be they for sex or shoes, car or companion. It has been said that many fine romances are wrecked by marriage. That could be turned around to say that many potentially good marriages are ruined by an unreal emphasis on romance. If a marriage has been based on a need for quick sexual love, chances are awfully good that it won't work out. There might also be a problem if each partner believes that the other is heaven-sent, capable of satisfying every need.

The truth of the matter is that there are countless individuals who could make us happy. The difficulty, sometimes, is finding them. Belief in a one and only, a Mr. or Ms. Right, is not only a futile exercise in itself, but it is behind many of the disappointments in love and marriage. So, too, is marrying to get away from family duties or a nagging parent. Marriage ought not to be viewed as an escape, as a means of easing pain. Marriage has its own special problems and struggles, not the least of which is that it is not, when you examine it carefully, a truly natural state. In fact, while monogamy is common in nearly all species of birds, it is rare, in general, among mammals — the group of animals that includes us.

But humans do choose to marry, and they share their lives with others, and they promise to remain sexually faithful. It is, certainly, a difficult way of life even under ideal circumstances. It is least of all always the way it is depicted in the magazine advertisements of smiling family members who play billiards, gather at outdoor barbecues, or sit before the fireplace reading together. Such ads are certainly based on the occasional events in our lives, and while they may be fine for selling pool tables, charcoal briquettes or books, they are not wholly realistic portrayals of family life.

The picture of marriage should not be a bleak one. Marriage can and does work. But it cannot be said strongly enough that marriage is, in the words of the psychologists, an interactive system in which the behavior of one member affects and is affected by the behavior of the other. It is two people giving of themselves, emotionally and physically, to one another. It is not merely taking or using. It may mean accepting and adjusting to the weaknesses and habits of the other.

You may not appreciate your partner's dietary habits, his or her friends or political views, but you learn to ignore them, not to let them trouble you; maybe you even learn to like them a bit. In a marriage one doesn't have to give up individual rights, desires and goals. It should not be said merely that marriage is "a great institution, but it ties me down."

We do change psychologically in marriage as we begin to play the parts of husband and wife, father and mother. Marriage does give our personalities a chance to develop. But we remain persons, individuals; and no contract, no religious ceremony, can change that. Accepting and adjusting and sharing do not mean that you lose your personal identity, the tag that makes you special. These things can, in fact, strengthen your identity, give it more character. On occasion, though, you may have to play down what it is that you want to do or what you believe. This is true in marriage and in any other close relationship. A baby cries at 4:00 A.M. and your wife, who usually feeds the child, isn't feeling all that great. You have to get up in an hour to be at work on time. The baby needs to be fed, so you make a concession and you get up, even though you'd like that extra hour of sleep. Or, your husband wants to watch a Sunday football game on television. You want to go for a quiet drive in the country with him. You are faced with two choices, as is he. You can sit and watch TV with him, or you can go on the drive alone. He can decide to give up the television and go on the drive with you, or stay home. Sometimes it is good for you to give in. Not all the time, because you don't want someone making your decisions for you all through life. But there are times when the expression "If the mountain won't come to Mohammed, Mohammed must go to the mountain" should be applied. Oftentimes, as in the case of the drive versus the football game, the couple compromises — that is, they agree together on one course of action. You take the drive alone, and he watches television, with the stipulation that you get together later and go to a movie.

The partners in a successful marriage, then, as well as those in a successful nonmarriage, are those who have learned how to function after the music stops, after romance and its heart-tripping frenzy has cooled. Everyone's heard that love can't last forever, and this is true simply because you don't live forever. But love does often last a lifetime, although its nature changes over the years. Margaret Reedy of the University of Southern California has studied this idea of loving happily ever after and the age differences in satisfying love relationships. She chose 102 married couples for her study. They were people who had been judged by others who knew them well to be very much in love. They were divided into three groups: young adults, married an average of five years; middle-aged adults, married an average of twenty-one years; and older adults, married an average of thirty-seven years. Each of the satisfied lovers was asked to complete a list of statements, rating each in terms of how well it described his or her current love relationship. These statements reflected a wide variety of possible experiences people might have in love relationships, and in turn reflected the six components of love we mentioned earlier (emotional security, referring to feelings of trust, caring, concern and warmth; respect, which means being able to be tolerant, understanding and patient; the ability to spend time together, working as well as playing; communication, being able to be honest and self-revealing, and being a good listener; loyalty, or a sense of investment and commitment; sexual intimacy).

What were the results of the survey?

There was, first of all, a clear indication that the nature of love in satisfying relationships is different at different ages. For example, the couples who assessed their current love alliance supported the common idea that passion and sexual intimacy are relatively more important in *early adulthood,* whereas tender feelings of affection and loyalty are more important in the love relationships of later life. The findings also supported the notion that, over time, love associations are less likely to be based on intense companionship and communication, and more likely to be based on tradition, commitment and loyalty. In addition to these explanations, Reedy found what she called "generational differences." "The belief that love means loyalty and being able to depend on one another is likely to be most consistent with the attitudes and beliefs of today's older generation," she observed. "By contrast, while today's young adult lovers place considerable emphasis on honest communication and self-disclosure in relationships, they are less likely to emphasize loyalty or long-term commitment to a relationship."

Reedy summarized her study this way:

The findings suggest that love can last a lifetime, but that the nature of love may be transformed by time. What these findings suggest is that passion, intense communication and self-disclosure are most important to affectionate bonding and love early in a relationship, while the sense of tenderness, emotional security, loyalty and commitment develop more slowly over time. In short, love relationships become less passionate but more tender, secure, comfortable and committed as lovers grow older together.[1]

While the study did show that passion is less important to late-life love and that the "softer" side of love is relatively more important, this does not mean that sexual passion necessarily dies after two people live together for a long time and fall into a calmer routine.

Sex, as we have said, is a powerful biological force, and sexual feelings will be with everyone throughout their lives, whether they're teenagers or well into their nineties. In fact, as couples grow older, sexual relations sometimes are vital to the strength of their marriage. Unfortunately — and this is a good place to inject this observation — it is not always easy for young people to understand the sexual nature of the very old, even of parents who may not be senior citizens. Although it is a fact that sexual activity and interaction are important in making the aging process easier to tolerate, the notion is widespread that sex is only for "the young," whatever that nebulous collective noun is supposed to mean. There are even jokes that focus on the lack of opportunity for sexual contact. The eighty-year-old woman complained to a neighbor that she couldn't sleep because a man kept banging on her door. "Why not open it?" the neighbor asked. "What, and let him out?" the woman replied. Even Napoleon is said to have complained, "At fifty, one can no longer love." Worse yet is the disapproving attitude of sons and daughters whose aged parents, left without spouses through death or divorce, begin to date again. The reason behind such a negative response might have as much to do with the way we generally regard our elderly as it does with our strange and often misguided views about sex. We should realize that while the ovaries (the female reproductive glands) and the sperm-producing cells of the male slow down and quit, the libido, or sex drive, does not.

We should stress here that a sexual relationship doesn't have to mean intercourse, either for young people or for a couple married a long time. In some marital therapy sessions — counseling programs for individuals who are having difficulty making their marriage work — there is an emphasis on exchanging affection by touching, cuddling and caressing. Says Dr. Harold Lief, an authority on sex and marriage, "The sense of touching is really underdeveloped in most of us. We have been misled by some Freudian doctrine in regard to this. Freud has given us the notion that the only mature kind of sexuality is [one pertaining to intercourse] and that all other aspects of sexuality are, in essence, infantile and immature. I want to emphasize that we really have to turn this about."

Let's return, for a moment, to that other requisite for getting along with people, communication. In the discussion of jealousy, it was said that it's not a good idea to assume your partner always knows what you're thinking. The importance of talking over what troubles or pleases us about a relationship was also discussed. Too many married couples suffer in silence, never talking over their needs or their feelings. Anger and frustration build up, and one day it all explodes, touched off, oftentimes, by an insignificant event or remark. Unkind words are exchanged, the situation gets out of hand, and someone walks out, sometimes for good, maybe without even knowing why. The person who is left behind also may not be able to identify the real problem. Sometimes, too, as the pent-up emotions become heavier, instead of bursting out in a rage, they mire the husband or wife in a deep depression from which he or she finds it difficult, if not impossible, to emerge without drugs or psychotherapy. Alcoholism and suicide, both a high price to pay, often go hand in hand with depression. Close friendship, understanding and a kindred spirit in whom one can confide are essential to emotional stability in such cases. If a husband or wife is not able or willing to lend the necessary support by talking out a problem, by being sensitive to the situation, a spouse's depression may not only worsen but a resentment can build up over the situation that has "ruined the marriage." Someone has to be blamed. "It's your fault," is the angry charge so often heard.

An interview I conducted with a woman a few years ago points up the difficulty some people have in communicating. I had asked the woman, who had a serious heart condition, if she talked much about her problem at home. "I do," she replied, "but I don't think they like me to. It upsets my son and husband. I knew I was having trouble before they diagnosed me, but I'd never admit it, and I hate to admit that I'm sick. Well, my husband would say to his friends, when they'd ask about me, 'Oh, she's okay, she's not too bad,' things like that. And after the first big attack, he'd say to people, 'Oh, she's a lot better today,' and I knew I wasn't. And that kind of irked me. Because, you see, I wanted sympathy, plain and simple, just some of that old tender, loving care, I'll admit. I do a little work, three nights a week, at a greeting card shop, and maybe that's why I go to the job. The manager is a nice man, and he's very sympathetic and so on. And he's worried about me. I think that's why I go to work when I know I shouldn't be going. Sympathy, pure and simple, what I wasn't getting at home. They just don't want to face the fact that I'm in trouble."[2]

Telling people that they ought to be more sympathetic and should communicate more is one thing. Actually putting communication into practice is difficult for some. Everyone knows how hard it is to pretend that nothing has happened, or to go on laughing when you've just had an argument with someone. Sometimes you need a cooling-off period to think out what's happened, to let some of the tension out. Sometimes you need a mediator, someone to make peace between you and your friend. A mediator does the communicating for you, telling your friend the things you should be telling him or her, bringing information from your friend to you. Married couples in difficulty often seek out a mediator, the counselor who tries to get them started again on an equal footing. Husband and wife may be asked to present their own views of what has gone wrong with the marriage, to discuss how they began going together, to share good memories and bad ones. Sometimes what each says hasn't been said for a long time, or maybe it's never been said. Each learns how the other assesses the marriage, what it has done for or to the partners. With time, and if the partners are serious about making their relationship work, deep-seated conflicts are brought into the open, a communication link is established, and marital harmony may be restored.

The advice of Dorothy Barash of the Menninger Memorial Hospital is well taken, whether we are married or contemplating it or just going together:

It is true we cannot change what has happened in the past, but we can try to understand it. We can free long-repressed rage and resentment by talking about it, acknowledging the hurts and feelings the spouse may not have known about. The process of talking over the hurt and being listened to, and perhaps finally feeling understood, is a form of catharsis which in itself is therapeutic. Once the past is looked at, a communication block often is removed. Then renegotiation can take place with the task of exploring vital questions: Where do we go from here? How can we make our marriage more meaningful for both of us?[3]

On the other hand, Barash wisely points out that some marital conflicts cannot be solved, despite well-meaning attempts at reconciliation or compromise. Whatever it is that prevents the couple from getting along may be just too serious for the marriage.

If the couple decides to separate on the basis of realistic incompatibility it should not be viewed as treatment failure. It takes courage to acknowledge one's inability (or unwillingness) to compromise values and to decide not to continue in a relationship which (because of the mate's rigidity, dependency, duplicity, infidelity, power struggle or whatever) is eroding one's personal identity and self-esteem. Dissolution of a hopeless marriage can be a constructive experience for both if they understand the rational reasons the marriage terminated. Examining and trying to understand the old hurts, accusations and sessions of anger which, at the time, seemed like open-heart surgery, can at least decrease the sometimes inordinate sense of failure and guilt and can lead to insight and growth.[4]

Which brings us to divorce, the dissolution of a marriage. Except under the laws of Islam — which permit a husband to divorce a wife simply by saying "I divorce thee" on three separate occasions and providing her with adequate financial assistance — obtaining a divorce is generally an involved procedure. In the United States, it requires a decree from a court of law.

Husband or wife may begin a divorce proceeding on various grounds. These include adultery, desertion, nonsupport, incurable insanity, imprisonment for life, "mental cruelty," or "incompatibility." Some states have a more liberalized "no-fault" divorce law whereby the petitioner need not lay any blame on his or her partner.

Attitudes toward divorce also differ. The Roman Catholic Church, for instance, is strongly opposed to divorce, holding that marriage is indissoluble, a sacrament from Christ as well as a lawful agreement. Some Catholics, of course, do not agree and have broken with their church to divorce and even marry again. Many other religions, however, hold that marriage is primarily a civil contract that may be broken for sufficient reason. But whatever the attitude toward it, it is a rare divorce that does not cause some emotional trauma and bitterness, particularly when children are involved. The mate who presses for divorce often feels guilty, and the partner who may not want divorce can feel rejected.

There is no question that divorce has increased over the years. In 1860, the divorce rate in the United States was 0.2 per one thousand population. That amounted to only a few thousand individuals. Today, one out of three American marriages ends in divorce. There are many reasons for this. Central to all of them, however, is that although the early needs of newlyweds have always changed through the years of marriage, today there is more openness in expressing new wants, more acceptance of them, and more opportunities for realizing them. There is a strong trend toward self-realization, a healthy desire for personal growth and self-reliance and for more freedom from the traditional possessiveness of marriage. The roles of men and women have changed dramatically, and only a few misdirected husbands still adhere to the Napoleonic Code of 1804, which advised, "Women, like walnut trees, should be beaten every day." Today, women can find employment in positions denied them in the past because they were women, or they can take advantage of educational opportunities that also were for men only. Today it is not uncommon to hear of husbands who take over all the domestic chores or at least share in "women's work." And today, with more modern birth control methods, women can expect, and rightfully so, sexual gratification that was also reserved for men, because the fear of pregnancy is eliminated.

As commendable as this modern picture may be, there are prices to pay. The problem may be that a husband and wife are not in agreement about how even a modern marriage should work. That is, one may be ready for a role reversal, or for more freedom from the other, before the other is. The solution may be to get out of the marriage. (It is interesting to note here that despite the high divorce rate, the number of remarriages among divorced people is very high. Some sociologists see this as proof that we are not so much dissatisfied with the institution of marriage as we sometimes are with our partners. In any event, more than 95 percent of the population marries, certainly no sign that marriage is a dying way of life.)

Consider this example of two people's not agreeing how a marriage should work. Suppose a woman is offered a full-time career position that requires a good deal of travel, business trips that will take her away from home for a week every month or two. She wants the job. Suppose her husband cannot accept the idea of his wife's working. He feels that her place is at home and that even though the kids are in school most of the day they still need her around. Moreover, although his own job hasn't involved travel, he has the idea that business trips are wild times on the road, full of hotel parties, sex and liquor. The alternatives are fairly clear. The woman can turn down the job, a move that would make her mate happy, but probably not her. On the other hand, she could take the job, making it quite clear that she has a right to a life outside the home. There is no question that either choice would put a strain on the marriage. The woman might feel resentful for having to give in to her husband, or guilty if she took the job against his wishes. The man might be angry or depressed if she took the job. He could become vindictive, and in an effort to punish his wife, might turn to another woman. Both, in the end, could demand a divorce.

But it need not end that way — provided there is some honest communication, and provided, of course, that the partners want to make things work the best way possible. A solution to the situation described is highly individual. The woman might become honestly convinced, after thinking it over, that it would not be in the best interests of the marriage for her to take the job at this time, and that although she wants the job, she will put her husband and the relationship first. The husband could realize that his wife does indeed have a right to the same things he does; that her being away might be inconvenient and mean a loss of companionship, but that it might also mean growth for both of them.

Recently, two male members of the Harvard Medical School faculty, themselves married to psychiatrists, took a close look at career marriages and scrutinized their own feelings as well as those of the other professional couples they examined. Some of the men questioned by Drs. Leon Eisenberg and Theodore Nadelson still felt annoyed at times, or were angry when a woman's professional duties bent the household out of shape. And there were indications that the deeply felt, long-standing belief that the wife has "executive responsibility" for the family chores is still with us.

Eisenberg and Nadelson also found that parents are readily manipulated by children who tend to measure parental performance by conventional standards. In a situation where a mother's absence at work draws complaints from a child, the father who shares that complaint is part of a conspiracy to play on the mother's guilt. Nonetheless, the two researchers felt that although stereotypes about the professional woman's status still persist, the tipping point has been reached. Moreover, they believe it will be the unpaid housewife, not the working wife, who will soon feel social pressure to justify her role. They concluded with this reassuring personal statement:

> We've had, and continue to have, a quite extraordinary experience in marriage, not one we were perceptive enough to seek when we fell in love. Nor yet one we welcomed fully when its depth first became manifest, but one with unique meaning for our own growth — the experience of living with a complete woman. Along the way, we may have surrendered the customary conveniences with some lack of grace. Yet in return we have been granted a love the richer and fuller for having its roots in mutual respect and growing maturity. That, we acknowledge, we owe our wives. Had it not been for their capacity to insist on respect for their integrity, it is doubtful we would have achieved what we now enjoy. We consider ourselves the most fortunate of men.

But what of the marriages that are not so fortunate, the ones that end in divorce and cannot be helped by counseling? Most people who divorce go through all manner of agonies, in com-

bination or alone — depending on whether they sought the un-
coupling or were asked for it — anger, depression, guilt, regret,
loneliness, and feelings of rejection and failure. For some, the
ordeal is a shattering one from which they never recover. They
may shun help, or be unaware it is available, and spend the rest
of their lives quite unhappily. Contributing to this unhappiness,
often, is that fact that the former mate is still a part of their
lives, whether near or far, and may be a constant source of sore
memories. Many other divorced people, on the other hand, are
able to work out their problems, drawing on inner strengths or
joining groups to share their experiences with people who have
been through it all themselves. If they have enough time, if they
are given enough help and understanding, they eventually
realize that they are not abnormal, that they are not alone, and
that quite possibly they can pick up the pieces and begin a better
life, remarried or single. The end of a marriage does not at all
mean that life, too, is at an end. In that light, divorce may be
seen as a positive growing experience, not only a way out of a
possibly unbearable situation but another chance to learn how
to love again.

But what about children? What about the effects a divorce
has on the sons and daughters of a husband and wife who cannot live together any longer? They undoubtedly have been
angry and bitter. They've felt depressed, rejected and scared.
Sometimes they may have tried to patch things up themselves,
or maybe bargained with their parents, promising one thing or
another if they'd just stick together. These are normal feelings
and they are there after any loss, whether it be a death in the
family or a loss of a job or a favorite friend. With time and
with the right supports, they are usually resolved.

Sociologists also have mixed ideas about whether divorce has any long-lasting effects on children. For years it was believed that a split home had to have a disastrous effect on them. Schizophrenia, for example, a severe emotional disorder whose most noticeable symptom is withdrawal from reality, has long been blamed on childhood disturbances and a bad family environment. The accepted theory has been that something is wrong between the child and his or her mother and father, or between the mother and father, and because of this adverse relationship the child's emotions and personality do not develop normally. The child grows up with this flaw, and when a crisis strikes — even a minor one — something gives way and the child becomes schizophrenic. The personality defect has made him or her vulnerable. Other studies have indicated that the children of broken homes are more apt to run afoul of the law, or do poorly in school.

On the other hand, a number of studies show no significant difference in any area of personality development between children from broken and unbroken homes. Remember that it is a serious mistake to take any one explanation, heredity or environment, and accept it as *the* answer to why we behave the way we do. If we accepted the schizophrenia argument fully, without considering other possibilities, we might conclude that everyone with an unfavorable home environment is or could be schizophrenic. And, as we know, that is not the case. Again, it is a combination of factors — social, biological, and psychological — that molds us.

Many mental health specialists believe it is probably better for the children of divorced parents to live with one parent, with a parent and grandparents or with a parent and a stepfather or stepmother, than with both parents who are continually quarreling and who have little love left for one another.

In other words, keeping a marriage together just for the children's sake may not necessarily be the right course. A family atmosphere charged with emotion and conflict is not very conducive to personal growth and development.

There is no doubt we live in a very different world from the one of a few generations ago. The emphasis on self-realization and the role changes men and women are experiencing have been mentioned. Women want their opinions taken seriously, as they should be, and are sharing more in decision-making in their private lives and on their jobs. Unfortunately, they often still must demand the equality that is inherently theirs. And men no longer are forced — or let's say that there's more awareness that they shouldn't be forced — to play the domineering male role. Although many men still do, of course, there is more acceptance of the gentle male today. Not the pompous man of "good birth" and social position that is implied in the term "gentleman," but the man who is tender and considerate, gentle in every sense of that mild-sounding word.

All of which means that men and women today, young and old, are behaving differently in their relationships with each other. In some marriages, for instance, couples have learned to adjust their lives to new demands that are made on them in both their professional and personal lives. They may worry about losing their identity, a very real fear, as we have seen, in a close relationship. Too much togetherness, we know now, is not healthy. Couples may understand and feel the need for variety in their lives, for friends of the opposite sex. A wife may see nothing wrong with having lunch or supper, without the excuse of business, with a male friend. A husband may want to have a drink with a female friend, or go to the movies with her on occasion. If a husband and wife are secure in their relationship they can handle such situations very well. Sometimes, couples carry their freedom to the extreme of having sex with others. Or, they join organizations of "swingers," a term used to identify those who regularly swap husbands and wives for sex.

It is up to the marriage partners to decide on whether they want their marriage to be an exclusive union or one that leaves room for other relationships. They must also decide on the degree of freedom each will be allowed. Some couples might agree on freedom to do exactly what each wants, conscience being the only guide. They might decide that whatever each wants to do and does will be kept secret from the other. Others may agree on total freedom with the provision that they will talk about their outside relationships only if they feel like it. Still others may draw up a list of dos and don'ts, either leaving it up to the individual to decide whether to talk about other lovers, or making it mandatory that the spouse "confess" if a rule is broken. They may even do this sort of thing if they're planning marriage, in what is known as contract marriage. In such an arrangement, the partners agree in advance on their individual rights and obligations. The contract might then come up for renewal every few years, and the partners are then supposed to decide whether to continue on as before, add or subtract rights and duties, or call an end to it all.

More common than contract marriage, however, is living together without marrying. According to the U.S. Census Bureau, some two million Americans have chosen this alternative way of life.

There are many reasons why couples decide to live this way. Two people fall in love and want to spend as much time together as possible. There may be an economic reason, the idea that two can live as cheaply as one. Many elderly couples, in fact, choose to live together for that reason. Some people simply cannot live by themselves, and need companionship. Some aren't sure that they want to marry each other, or even ever marry anyone, so they live together in what they regard as a trial marriage, one in which they can get to know each other better. "We just want to see what it would be like together for a while," said one young couple. "We've learned a lot so far about ourselves as individuals, and about how we are together. We don't know when we'll get married, but at least we don't think we'll be making a mistake if we decide on that." A young man put it in stronger terms: "You wouldn't buy a car before trying it, would you?" It does appear, if one can believe the spot surveys of college students that have been conducted throughout the country, that a high percentage of them at least say that they eventually want to marry — if not their current partner, then someone else, before they are too old. The situation, thus, may be the same as for the divorced person who remarries — it isn't the institution of marriage that is rejected but the wrong partner.

Other couples have no plans to marry, and they simply live together because they oppose the institution for personal reasons. They may have been through a bad marriage, and have lost faith in the institution; they don't want to make the same mistake again. They may consider marriage an unnatural lifestyle that stifles the participants; they may not want the immense responsibility of raising a family, maintaining a home, and working all at the same time, which marriage often entails; they may be emotionally immature, too dependent on family to really break away by marrying formally; or they are bothered by the fact that they'll never find the ideal mate, so they've made up their minds never to marry.

There are, of course, advantages and disadvantages in living together without legal marital ties. If the couple is mature enough to understand that there is more to it all than being able to have sex whenever they want, that they may learn more about one another and whether or not they want to spend a lifetime together, then the arrangement may be worthwhile. In this regard, it may well be that living together is another step in the courtship process, which begins when boy meets girl. There is also an advantage in being able to date others without being hung up by a traditional marriage, which forbids such behavior. This, however, has to depend on the nature of the relationship, on the ground rules that the couple has laid down. Finally, either one of the pair can walk out at any time without any legal obligations. (This may be changing. In December 1976, the California Supreme Court gave legal status to living together. It ruled that if two unmarried persons agree to share property acquired by them while they live together, then that agreement, verbal or implied, is as valid as if they were married. Because of that decision, actor Lee Marvin was sued for $1.8 million by the woman who lived with him for several years. After a lengthy trial, the woman, Michelle Triola Marvin, was awarded $104,000 — approximately equal to the amount she had earned as a singer for two years.)

The disadvantages generally have to do with how others view the arrangement. For instance, your parents might not approve of your moving in with someone of the opposite sex, and if you're a young woman you may find they disapprove even more. One woman in her early twenties moved into an apart-

ment with her male friend. They were planning to marry —
and did a few months later — but to keep the peace they put
only her name on the mailbox. He had a mail address at a
friend's. There were two telephones with different numbers in
the apartment, one for him, one for her. Neither would answer
the other's. Whenever their parents planned to visit — fortu-
nately both their mothers and fathers lived out of state and
never paid any surprise visits — one or the other would move in
with a friend, taking all clothing and personal belongings along.
"We'd even hide the other phone under the bed," said the
woman.

But it's not only parents who might look with disfavor at the
arrangement. Landlords and landladies often object on moral
grounds, and there are some who won't even allow a member of
the opposite sex to visit a tenant alone. Moreover, since cohabita-
tion is not generally dealt with officially, couples cannot take
advantage of the many benefits the law accords those who are
legally married. Joint ownership of property, income tax com-
putation, survivor's benefits, even the legal status of a child
born to an unmarried couple are things not easily dealt with in
the absence of a marriage license. Undoubtedly, this will change
as more and more couples decide on trial marriages, or simply
want to live together. The fact of the matter is, you don't lose
your individuality or your civil rights merely because you decide
to move in with someone.

Is there any difference, then, between living together and
being married, since couples often give similar reasons for en-
tering either one or the other arrangement?

Some might argue that there is, indeed, a great difference,
that unmarrieds have much more personal freedom and are
not as bound to do what society expects of married partners.

Whether this is true depends, of course, on why the couple decides to live together in the first place. If it's simply an economic arrangement, then chances are the partners will live their own lives pretty freely outside the home. If they've moved in together because each excites the other sexually, then they'll probably stay together until that wears off, and then move on to another romantic high with someone else; the idea being to sustain a level of passion that cannot be sustained over years with the same person. In cases like these, the commitment to live together is made because of what the partners can get from one another. As the song says, "It was great fun, but it was just one of those things." The actual relationship may not be as important as the convenience. If this is true, then living together is different from what marriage is — or, let's say, what it should be. On the other hand, if two people are genuinely interested in each other, and decide to live together to get to know each other better, to determine if marriage will work out, then their commitment must be stronger. They will experience jealousy; they must learn to fight possessiveness and to allow varying degrees of personal freedom. They must work at the relationship, just as though they were married. And, if they decide to split, the break will be as emotion filled as it would be if they were formally married. It cannot be any other way, if the partners truly care for one another at the outset, if they communicate and share.

The decision to move in with the person you love is not an easy one to make. Besides the disadvantages already mentioned, there is often a nagging doubt about its real value. Can you really know a person better by living with him or her for a few months or a year? Isn't going together exclusively the same thing? Even couples who have been married for several years aren't sure about each other. Claude Lelouch, the French film director, is one who knows a good deal about love and marriage, both on and off the screen. "I've lived with women since I was eighteen," he told a reporter recently. "I've been married ten times. When you love, you always think it will last forever." Does the ease with which one can get out of the arrangement help or hinder? Certainly the stigma of divorce is not present if the couple splits, nor is there any concern over having failed in the eyes of those who appreciate the stability and legitimacy of marriage. But, if John knows he can leave Sue anytime he chooses, and vice versa, what does this do to commitment, which is what love is all about? Can one be truly committed if the relationship is open ended?

There are no simple answers to such questions. But you should discuss them and try to answer them. One thing should be said, and that is that divorce, nontraditional marriages and living together do not spell the end of society and the family. Families will always be with us, and not only because we need them to survive biologically. They are the core of civilization, the nucleus of our social organization. They enable us to be secure, to enjoy companionship, and to express affection and friendship. Without families, most human activities would be like a deflated balloon, lacking in both substance and appeal.

But times change, and so do our needs. And with these shifts will come changes, one hopes healthier ones, in marriage, in family structure and in the way we choose to live together. Apart from the alternatives already mentioned, there are, for example, communes, groups of unrelated individuals who live together as families. In 1965, there were an estimated one hundred communes in the United States, and some three thousand in 1971. Moreover, according to a recent youth-attitude survey conducted by the Institute of Life Insurance, there is an indication that more than a third of the fourteen- to twenty-four-year-olds feel that a communal way of living may become a common alternative to traditional family life. A group of Rutgers University sociologists who studied young people living together found that three reasons brought unrelated people into arrangements usually reserved for families—a desire for personal growth, an attempt at more practical living arrangements and/or a rejection of society. Others have suggested that communal living may be a way of extending the American nuclear family, which has become increasingly smaller as parents and grown children tend to live apart. In line with this, the Reverend James L. Gibbons, director of chaplaincy for the University of Chicago Hospitals and Clinics, told a meeting of the American Medical Association that small families place extra-heavy demands on the marital partners to meet each other's needs singly.

Marriage is not always a feather bed, nor does it necessarily become any softer with time. But when it is strong, as that great repository of Jewish tradition, the Talmud, holds, a couple could sleep together on a sword's blade. When it is weak, however, a bed of sixty cubits is not wide enough.

8

Sex Education

CONTACT WITH OTHER HUMAN BEINGS and experience are, as we all know, the best of teachers. Add in books and teachers, and we can learn a good deal about human nature and about ourselves. But when it comes to sex, there seems to be a problem. Most parents are not going to tell you that you ought to learn about sex through experience. And many more are afraid that if you learn about it from teachers, in sex education classes, it'll put nasty ideas in your head.

A few years ago, after the appearance of a newspaper article I had written about a community sex-information service, I received the following letter from an irate reader:

Now in the twentieth century, lewd, indecent and sick minds write dirty sexual novels, all for money. Producers present nude sexual plays, all for money. Organizations like yours are talking sex, sex, sex, all for money. Other sick minds like yours advocate free love and premarital sex relations so little bastards can be born with no respect or legal claims to anything. You should all be placed in a compound and separated from people who respect the morals and decency that civilization has developed over the years.

The writer, like most who send such letters to newspapers, did not sign his or her name. The letter was simply signed, "One of Many."

Whoever wrote that letter is, indeed, one of many. He or she is always there, you may be sure, whenever certain "taboo" subjects are raised. If a young person mentions sex education, alcohol, death, crime and violence, alternative life-styles, drugs and all the rest of those "awful" subjects, these people panic. If they don't remain silent — which is one way those who cannot deal with such subjects respond — they let young people know, and quite forcefully, that they're too young to talk about such things or, in the case of drinking and sex, that they shouldn't do either, period. Once, at a church meeting, I suggested to parents that it was better to communicate about death with a child than to maintain a conspiracy of silence, that children do think about death, whether adults believe it or not, and that they are affected by it. I said that my book on death for young readers included discussions of murder and suicide, and talked about some of the reasons why people kill others and themselves. When I was through, a woman got to her feet and told me angrily, "You should have your head examined, telling kids that sort of stuff. You'll give them ideas." My answer was, "I hope so."

The attitude of that woman in the audience is even more common when it comes to sex education. Many adults even today would find pleasing the remarks of one clergyman who wrote on "sex education" many years ago. "It is necessary to warn the boy against masturbation without running the risk of teaching the sin by explaining the manner of committing it," said the priest. He added this word of warning: "In giving sex education to the young, we should never bring out the fact of the pleasure associated with sexual acts. The mind may eventually be debauched."

That kind of advice, well-intentioned though it may have been, does more damage than good because it is based on a misguided morality, on a notion of sex as evil, rather than on truth. It is not necessary or advisable to warn anyone against masturbation. Stimulating one's own genitals is quite normal, and most, if not all, physicians will tell you it does absolutely no harm whatsoever. In fact, it may relieve sexual tension that can build up and sometimes cause physical and emotional problems. And as for not mentioning the pleasure of sex, equating this pleasure with later debauchery is like saying that if we so much as touch a drop of liquor we will become alcoholics. It could be argued that the person who gives out such advice is the one actually committing the wrong. Such advice can easily trap a young man and woman in a net of guilt and anxiety that will hold and trouble them all their lives.

This leads to the purpose of this chapter. Most young people have had some sex education in school or under the direction of a church or community organization. A few may even have had some such explanation at home. Sometimes the sex education courses tell a good deal about how to prevent pregnancy, about condoms, diaphragms and oral contraceptives. Students may see films of couples engaging in sexual intercourse, or they may hear a lecture by a homosexual or a prostitute. Other sex education courses are a bit more timid, and they focus only on anatomy, on the various sexual organs and their names. Some may even avoid the word *sex* in the title, preferring softer-sounding names like "Personal Development" or "Family Life." Sex education may simply be part of a biology course, where the discussion tends to focus on red and green algae, earthworms, cells and microbes, but rarely on how sexual human beings fit into the scheme.

Whether they be good ones or bad ones, the courses are being offered, and in addition many adequate books are available. So, no sex information will be presented in this chapter, which will instead discuss sex education itself—what it should be, how some adults view it, the disagreements and controversies that are associated with it, and some of the problems that a lack of it can create. After all, the argument's outcome will affect the future, so everyone ought to be informed enough about the subject to express an intelligent opinion. How much sex education ought to be taught, by whom and how?

Begin by considering the recent reasoning of a policy committee of the National Assessment for Education Progress. It made a decision to omit questions about birth control, venereal disease and reproduction from a government-sponsored survey that was administered to seventeen-year-olds! The sex-related questions, according to one report, were not asked because the policy committee felt they were "too controversial." The questions were put, however, to young adults twenty-six to thirty-five years old.

Teenagers might well raise an eyebrow or two at the decision. The following facts about that age group make it almost ludicrous:

◆ Nearly all teenagers will have engaged in some sort of intimate sexual activity — from heavy petting to "going all the way" — by the time they're nineteen. Although it is difficult to determine just how many teenagers have had sexual intercourse, family planning authorities know that the number is quite high, substantially higher, in fact, than it was only a few years ago. According to some experts, among the approximately ten million girls in the United States aged fifteen to nineteen, about 40 percent have had premarital sexual relations. And of these four million sexually active individuals, about 28 percent have become pregnant one or more times. (Another survey of fifteen hundred teens, thirteen to nineteen years of age, found that more than 60 percent of the girls and 70 percent of the boys were having intercourse regularly.)

✦ Of the million or so teenage girls who become pregnant every year, about six hundred thousand, according to the National Center for Health Statistics, will give birth. The others will end the pregnancy by abortion. Of the teenage girls who actually bear children, many will try to raise them alone or with the help of relatives, a few will work to support them, but the majority will depend on welfare. Others will place the children up for adoption.

✦ Venereal disease — except for the common cold and flu infections, the most common infectious disease in the United States — strikes primarily at teenagers and young adults. Actually a mixed bag of fourteen sexually transmissible diseases, of which syphilis and gonorrhea are the most serious, VD is epidemic in this country and in other parts of the world. There is little doubt in the minds of most public health officials that the birth control pill and changing attitudes toward sex are important reasons for the mass outbreak. (The pill is usually singled out for criticism because, while it is an extremely effective contraceptive, its chemical nature does little to ward off gonorrhea germs. Communicable diseases expert Dr. Nicholas J. Fiumara of the Massachusetts Department of Public Health points out that in the once widely used diaphragm-jelly method of birth control the jelly — which is designed to destroy sperm — is acidic. It sets up a chemical barrier to gonorrhea infection because the organism that causes the disease cannot survive in an acid medium. Dr. Fiumara explains that there is no acid barrier with the pill, and a woman using this method of contraception who is intimate with a man with gonorrhea has nearly a 100 percent chance of becoming infected.)

Consider VD among homosexuals. A lot of you probably don't know — and this includes your parents — that a good many physicians believe an increasing number of sexually transmitted diseases can be traced to contacts between male homosexuals. Moreover, many of the homosexuals themselves are not aware of the consequences of sexual promiscuity. And sometimes when they are concerned, according to a recent report in *American Medical News,* they hesitate to seek medical care because they fear the physician's disapproval.[1] Certainly sex education is important here, too.

Insofar as unwanted pregnancies are concerned, a 1976 survey demonstrated that although many teenagers use contraceptives effectively, more than three hundred thousand pregnancies could be avoided if the teens used birth control methods as regularly as they engaged in sex. According to the Johns Hopkins University physicians who conducted the study, some teenagers do not use contraceptives consistently because they may not appreciate the risk of pregnancy, or because they are uncomfortable seeking out birth control advice. Others may simply not know where to go for the necessary information.

Most people would agree that sex education that includes what used to be known as "the facts of life" — reproductive biology, how to prevent pregnancy and avoid disease — is imperative today, probably more than it ever was. Even some parents who are not generally happy with sex education outside the home have to admit that the epidemic of VD, pregnancy, illegitimacy and abortion is far worse than no information at all. Consider the problems that come with a teenage pregnancy. A 1978 report in the journal *Family Planning Perspectives* points out that the repercussions of teenage childbearing are long lasting.[2] The young parents usually drop out of school and thus get less education than their classmates who postpone childbearing; they are limited to less prestigious jobs, and the jobs landed by the young women, in particular, are classified as dead-end. The marriages of young people who become parents are rarely stable and are, with few exceptions, unhappy affairs.

Some young men are highly sensitive to the repercussions of getting a girl pregnant. They know that marriage means interrupting their educations and careers, but they feel it is the right thing to do. Others would argue that, since no one can prove the baby is theirs, the best thing to do is to deny it and forget all about it. A young woman might want to put the baby up for adoption or have an abortion, maybe without consulting the young father. Each of these courses of action can leave an emotional scar.

Sex education while you are young is also important to how well you adjust, socially and personally, as an adult. The wrong advice about sex can make you feel guilty. You may, for example, have committed some sexual act frowned upon by your parents or even by one of your friends. If you don't have the right information, it's only natural to feel anxious, even that you are a "bad" person. Chances are you'll work things out as you grow older, but there's always the possibility that if the guilt is irrational it will leave a mark on you that's hard to erase. This is not to suggest that without sex education everyone will turn into guilt-ridden individuals, never able to maintain a meaningful sexual relationship. Nor that if you repress your sexual nature you'll become a deviate.

Nevertheless, repressed and poorly shaped attitudes toward sexuality *do* play a part in many forms of deviant behavior. It has been suggested, for instance, that the *nymphomaniac* (a female with an abnormal desire for sexual intercourse, who is rarely satisfied) and her male counterpart, the man who suffers from *satyriasis,* may be individuals who feel inferior or guilty, and this prevents them from obtaining satisfaction. The *masochist,* too, the person who gains sexual pleasure from suffering, may be guilt-plagued, unconsciously welcoming punishment for his or her sins. Finally, the *exhibitionist,* the person who exposes his genitals, may be trying to demonstrate to himself or to others that he is not sexually inadequate. The female performer who strips on stage may also fit into this category.

Learning as much about sex as you can when you are young, then, is crucial. Not everyone, however, agrees with one Chicago physician, Dr. Lonny Myers of the Midwest Population Center, who said recently that the way to prevent teenage pregnancy is to begin teaching about sex in the second grade while the subject is as impersonal as grammar and long division. "Show them the pills, IUDs, condoms and diaphragms," she told an American Public Health Association news conference. "Birth control can and should be taught to second, third and fourth graders in terms of world population problems and in simple language. Withhold nothing. Teach them the facts when their own sexuality is not involved. Then when they're ready for sex, they'll have the background, the language and sophistication to accept what we say about responsible sex."[3]

The age at which sex education ought to be taught is not the only issue that is debated whenever the topic comes up. Other issues are how it will be taught, and by whom.

These are most difficult to resolve, and there are many opinions. They are difficult because one's personal ideas about sex and morality must be tied to them, and not everyone thinks the same way in such matters. For example, how much moral guidance — that is, how much emphasis on right and wrong — should be taught? Some people have strong ideas about that. They may feel that virginity, "saving yourself" sexually for the right person, usually with marriage in mind, is the most desirable goal, and they may emphasize that in teaching about sex. If so, they might also refuse to teach anything about the various methods of birth control because then students might want to know how to use them. Others, however, might believe that it is more irresponsible, or immoral, *not* to teach a young person how to prevent having an unwanted child. They argue that having sex is a perfectly natural act, that people can't really change their desire for sex, and that since they're going to do it anyway they'd better learn everything there is to know, so they'll handle it right. Some are convinced that sex, especially those aspects that deal with values and responsibility, should be taught in the home. Parents who prefer this approach may very well argue that they don't want anyone else's values thrust upon their children — and then they proceed to impose their own. On the other hand, some parents may genuinely want their children to decide for themselves what is responsible sexual behavior, and the best way to achieve this, they feel, is to present both sides at home. Some sex education courses might be too heavily weighted with birth control information and might not place enough emphasis on the fact that although sex is quite natural it is not the only element in our lives. Parents who have come to terms with their own sexuality, who are comfortable discussing it together and with their children, are undoubtedly the best teachers. But, and this is the argument of many who want sex education made available, the majority of parents are either unable to talk about sex, or in doing so they communicate misinformation and anxiety. Many clergymen, too, sex education proponents feel, give young people imperfect explanations of sexual behavior or overemphasize the moral and physical harm that may come with sex. Since the information generally received from friends "on the street" — unfortunately a common method of education and one that even some parents go along with because they are too embarrassed to talk about sex — is also flawed, this leaves the schools.

Unfortunately, the schools are not always the best ones to do the job either. Many sex educators are poorly trained. They may be pressed into part-time service, much as, say, a school might ask a science teacher to double as a basketball coach. Some are afraid. A reporter was preparing a newspaper article on sex education recently, and was asked by an officer of a state parent-teacher-student organization not to write about the subject. His excuse was that no one really cared about it. Said the officer: "A newspaper article could cause a serious step back and delay even longer the availability of needed information to our children, a terrible sacrifice for a subject really quite dull and passé." Another high school administrator pleaded: "Do you have to write about this? We don't want people to misunderstand. And please don't call it sex education. The name of the course is 'Parenting.'"

Worse, some teachers are not willing to let their students form opinions of their own, lecturing them, instead, on the dos and don'ts of sex. This last is unfortunate because in the end it is the individual who must decide what is responsible or irresponsible behavior. Teachers can give a lot of information, and they may even express opinions, but the student is the one who should ultimately make the choices. With enough information and discussion everyone will come to the "right" or "wrong" conclusions on his own and for himself.

9

Sex and Morality

THERE HAS BEEN a great deal of talk about the importance of being informed and about how sex education is essential to prevent unwanted pregnancies and venereal disease, and to learn how to have a healthy sex life. Obviously, sex education makes an assumption here. That is, many people will have sex before they marry. If no one thought that, there would be no reason to talk about birth control methods or about how to ward off a sexually transmissible disease.

Sometimes, sex education is offered wholeheartedly by individuals who condone premarital sex and who want everyone to be able to enjoy it without fear of having a child or contracting a serious illness. Sometimes the information is given grudgingly by individuals who do not condone premarital sex but who feel that since people probably will engage in it, it's better to be safe than sorry.

All this brings up one of the most important considerations in a book of this sort — the advisability and the morality of sex before marriage. There are two pressing questions to be asked: Should you? Is it right?

These questions are in the mind of everyone who is involved with sex education. But often the questions are not asked directly, and a student gets all the information he or she needs but little guidance about what to do with it, about whether it should or shouldn't be used.

There is no general agreement on whether young people should or should not have sex, about whether it is right or wrong. Many people will say that it is wrong, and that young people shouldn't. Sometimes this absolutist stand is based on strict religious teaching, on the traditional belief that sex and sin are synonymous. Such a viewpoint might cite the Bible, which tells us to "abstain from fleshly lusts which war against the soul." Or Saint Paul's stern warning: "For know you this and understand, that no fornicator, or unclean or covetous person hath inheritance in the kingdom of Christ and of God." For orthodox Christians, the pleasure of sex was put there by God to induce humans to continue the species so that it could, in turn, worship Him. It was not, they hold, instituted to be enjoyed for its own sake. Sometimes those who oppose premarital sex on religious grounds maintain that abstinence, except in marriage, purifies the soul and makes us better persons. By fighting and overcoming our animal instincts we demonstrate the use of consciences that make us different from and superior to animals, consciences that make us moral and give us human dignity. Some of the early church fathers even believed that married couples who enjoyed sexual relations were "befouling" an act that they had to concede was essential if the earth was to be populated. It was, in their minds, a necessary evil.

Other individuals are against having sex before marriage because such behavior might make it difficult for one to be sexually faithful in a marriage; the reason being that the couple that engages in premarital sex treats it lightly. Still others cite psychological studies showing that sex before marriage can cause guilt, which in turn adversely affects the sexual relationship of two people when they marry. And finally, there are those who oppose premarital sex for their daughters but not for their sons. The fact that someone else's daughter is having sex with a son is somehow ignored. Several states also apply this discriminatory double standard when considering the legality of sexual intercourse. For instance, they define intercourse between a married man and an unmarried woman as fornication, a minor offense; but intercourse between a married woman and an unmarried man is often defined as adultery, a more serious charge.

Proponents of sex before marriage do not see it as a moral issue but one to be decided by each individual. Others also wonder why, if sex was so horrid a crime, it is not mentioned specifically among the temptations that the New Testament tells us Christ was subjected to at the hands of the devil in the desert. Some may feel that premarital sex helps couples make an easier adjustment to sex in marriage because they will have experimented, maybe with different partners. They might, then, come to the right conclusions about what sex can and should not be. Finally, there is the argument that sexual release is important to your physical and mental health.

But before we go on, let's listen to what some young people say about it.

"Sex before marriage is absolutely necessary," observed one high school student. "Unless you want to gamble on your happiness for the rest of your life. Sex is so much more now than making babies. It is a time to give and share and enjoy the pleasure that your body can bring. Without experiencing sex before marriage, you could be ruining a perfect match. After all, we spend our days together, why not our nights?" Said another: "I don't think you should have sex completely unless you can make a commitment." A young man echoed that, saying, "It's okay if it's a good relationship, one that is planning to last." Commented another: "It depends on the person. In my case, I know it's all right because it's a terrific way of sharing something with someone you love. I've had sex with people I don't love but I'm not a nervous wreck about it, so it must be right for me." Another put it this way: "I think it's fine, but it should be something that is not planned. It should happen spontaneously. Two people will know when it's right for them, without even having to talk about it." And finally, consider this response from a young woman: "A physical relationship is beautiful, but it isn't what love is all about. If two people love each other so much that they are going to spend the rest of their lives together, whether they have great sex or not wouldn't change their decision to get married. So, I don't believe in the cliché that you wouldn't buy a pair of shoes without trying them on. People aren't shoes, and two people in love would be able to express physically their feelings for each other, one way or another. It probably sounds as though I believe that sex before marriage is wrong. I don't. I just don't think that marriage is about sex and people should be 'tried on.' I think the physical part of a relationship is wonderful and people shouldn't deprive themselves of this pleasure simply because they're not married. But sex is an adult responsibility, and should be handled as such. The two people should be prepared emotionally for the risks of pregnancy."

Everyone has something to say about it. And this, of course, can be confusing when it comes to determining what is appropriate behavior. When, really, is certain behavior wrong or right? Is there ever room for the word *sometimes?* Perhaps you've reasoned it's okay to have sex with someone because everything was just right, the music, no parents around, and because you both wanted to very much. You might feel that you have to make these decisions because of circumstances. Or, on the other hand, perhaps you've asked, "What will be the consequences of this if we go through with it? Will our relationship change? Will we feel guilty? Will we take each other for granted?" There are other questions to be asked. Should your sexual behavior be governed by what your parents think? Do you abstain because it will please them? Because it will please God? Do you have sex because all your friends are doing it? Do you avoid having sex because you're afraid? Because you value being a virgin?

It's not always easy to figure out what we should or should not do, and why. Sometimes the philosophy we hold today isn't so appealing tomorrow. We grow impatient with two opposing schools of thought that make so much sense on their own sometimes, but can't seem to be able to exist side by side. It's understandable, therefore, if we just want to forget it all — to long for some ironclad rule that would force us to behave one way or the other. That might uncomplicate matters. Or would it? Think about that. What it would mean, really, is that the decisions in this area of your life would always be made for you. More rules only mean less opportunity for the individual to choose.

Since this is a very personal matter, let me say here that I don't have all the answers either. But I do have some opinions, and I am comfortable, at least now, with them. You may agree or not. You may agree with me today but not next year. My views may not be those of your parents. I hope, though, that they'll make you think a little more deeply about the subject of sex, perhaps in a different way from how you feel now.

I can begin by making two statements. The first is that sex before you're married is not always wrong, no more than drinking or gambling or telling a lie are wrong in themselves. The second is that having sex is not the same as offering someone a handshake.

Let's take the first statement — that premarital sex is not always wrong. Sex is normal human behavior, a powerful drive that we are all born with, as natural as hunger and thirst. It enables us to bring new life into the world, and at the same time it is pleasurable. One cannot deny that we are often first attracted sexually to the one we decide to spend a good deal of time with, even our entire lifetime. Sex, also, is closely tied to our very vitality, our physical and mental vigor, our capacity to grow and create and act. Some would go so far as to say that without any sexual desire whatsoever, we become emotionally bankrupt, creatively snowbound.

It is not my intention to begin a debate over morality and sin. But I must make the point that sex, one of our great biological needs, ordained by God if you prefer, has been made "dirty" by humankind. It is not so in itself. An excellent example of this corrupting of sex appears in a book written more than seventy-five years ago by the psychologist Havelock Ellis: "In Japan, the bathing place of the women was perfectly open, and Englishmen were offered no obstacle nor excited the least repugnance; indeed, girls after their bath would freely pass, sometimes as if holding out their hair for innocent admiration, and this continued until countrymen of ours by vile laughter and jests made them guard themselves from insult by secrecy. So corruption spreads. . . ."[1]

I do not believe that every time you have sex before you marry that you are doing wrong or that you should be punished for it. For some, it has been and will be a good experience. The fact is, sex is normal; as we have said, it is a way of showing love (and that in itself is good), and of communicating. The lust that you feel before you have sex, that hunger to touch another and to be touched, that need for physical and emotional release, are normal, too. It is not, in my mind, "the beast within," as Freud put it, nor a demon that will necessarily drive us down the road to damnation. True, lust is listed as one of the Seven Deadly Sins, along with pride, envy, sloth, anger, avarice and gluttony. But lust, like all the other members of its centuries-old family, is something to be wary of, rather than something to feel guilty over when it hits you, as it will. It would be unrealistic for me to suggest that a sexual relationship without love can never be rewarding.

More about this later, but for the moment let's be honest and admit that sometimes we feel like indulging an appetite, and that after we have done what it is we wanted to do, we sometimes feel a lot better — not all the time, because we may feel guilty, but usually. "Human beings are simply not the kind of beings who always love the people they lust after," Dr. Albert Ellis, a psychotherapist and expert on human sexuality, once observed, "and to demand that they should do so is to help make them guilty and self-hating." At a meeting of students at Michigan State University several years ago, Dr. Ellis challenged a number of other objections to premarital sexual relations, saying that sex also "begets love," particularly in males, and that the sex act is immoral only when it needlessly and definitely harms oneself or another human being. And with regard to the argument that to desire someone solely for physical satisfaction is of the lowest animal nature, Dr. Ellis suggested that sexual enjoyment is hardly lower than the pleasures of eating, watching a sunset, hearing a symphony, or smelling a rose. Our ability to think rationally, said Ellis, makes it virtually impossible for us to be purely animalistic in any act.

Dr. Ellis's views are, of course, quite controversial, but it is important for you to know about them. You should also know that in his talk he pointed out that nearly everyone who advocates premarital sexual freedom wants our sex instincts to be tightly tied to honesty, considerateness, mutual consent and even love. "What we sexual libertarians invariably fight for is the removal of arbitrary, needless, foolish, anxiety-abetting and hostility-fomenting fetters on sex relations," he explained. "We do not want complete sex freedom, any more than we want removal of all restrictions on business transactions, on automobile driving, or on using murderous weapons."[2]

Which brings me to the second statement — that having sex is not the same as shaking hands. What this means, of course, is that sex is a strong force, a serious business not to be taken lightly — even though it's often done simply for fun. Besides the drawbacks we mentioned earlier — pregnancy and venereal disease — premarital sex raises another set of problems. I said earlier that having sex before you're married is not wrong all the time. Like everything else we do in life, however, it can be done in the wrong way and for the wrong reasons. The act of having sex is not wrong, no more than is the generation of nuclear energy or the manipulation of a gene in a laboratory or placing a bet on a football game. But while these things are not wrong in themselves, the potential for wrong is there, all the time. If, for example, your attitudes toward sex condone indulgence without considering the possible emotional harm you may be doing to yourself or others, the odds are fairly good that your attitude as an adult will be equally mechanical, because you have never really learned how to enjoy. Sexual partners can become mere objects to be used when convenient as a means to an end, to disguise a down moment, to supply a buzz just as liquor does.

I said before that the sex drive is instinctive, an urge that wants to be satisfied. That urge for physical release is a strong one, generally stronger when we are young. Some people are more sexually responsive than others for a wide range of reasons including our genetic makeup, and our upbringing. But all of us, young and old, learn to control our sexual urges to varying degrees depending, again, on our biological makeup, and on our cultural, emotional or religious environment. As a teenager, your sexual feelings may be stronger and your controls weaker than those of an adult, but only you can best determine how to exercise those controls. After all, you are in charge. You can choose to have sex or not. Although we compared the sex drive to eating and drinking, it's not exactly the same as feeling hungry for a meal or thirsty for a glass of water. If you pass up food and drink for very long, you'll become ill and die. That's not going to happen if you avoid sex.

If this talk about controls sounds a bit moralistic, it's meant to be. Though the act of having sex is not an immoral one, it is linked closely to the issue of morality, because when you have sex you're involving another human being. What you do will have an effect on others, as well as on yourself and your future behavior. It is the consequences of your actions that make human sexuality such an integral part of morality. We can no more ignore moral considerations when discussing sexuality than we can ignore alcoholism when discussing alcohol.

Not everyone agrees. There are still many people who regard sexual intercourse as simply a recreational act, like playing tennis or swimming. They look for different partners, as a surfer seeks the perfect wave, hoping that the next one will be better, that the blast will be bigger. Don Juan, a legendary Spanish pursuer of women, was such a person. Amoral in the true sense of the word, and reckless, his name is synonymous with casual sex. So, too, is the name of Casanova, an Italian adventurer, gambler and lover. The only rule some promiscuous individuals seem to be governed by is that as long as it makes you feel happy there's no problem. Or, as Ernest Hemingway put it when discussing morality, "What's moral is what you feel good after, and what's immoral is what you feel bad after."

Some of those who approach sex the way that Don Juan and Casanova did may have deep psychological problems. They may be unable to commit themselves to anyone in particular, or give totally of themselves, emotionally as well as physically, as sexual intimacy demands. A young man might seek the company of a prostitute or an acquaintance who is not particular about her sexual partners. A young woman might enter into a sexual relationship with a married man who has no intention of leaving his wife, content to be his mistress because she doesn't want the involvement of marriage. For some of these people, the sex act is not really much different from masturbating. There is, of course, sexual arousal followed by gratification, and that can be fun. But when it's over there is often an emptiness, a lack of any feeling for the partner. It is as though the partners were merely erotic pictures, capable of arousing fantasies but with no substance, certainly not enough to make them remember one another in a few weeks. Complete giving, which is what the sexual act is really all about, means complete in a broader sense, too — that is, fully carried out, thorough, and that entails something more than a one-night stand.

Henry Fairlie, a British journalist who has written on moral issues, observes:

> Lust dies at the next dawn and, when it returns in the evening, to search where it may, it is with its own past erased. Love wants to enjoy in other ways the human being whom it has enjoyed in bed. But in the morning Lust is always furtive. It dresses as mechanically as it undressed, and heads straight for the door, to return to its own solitude. Like all the sins, it makes us solitary. It is a self-abdication at the very heart of one's own being, of our need and ability to give and receive. . . . If people now engage in indiscriminate and short-lived relationships more than in the past, it is not really for some exquisite sexual pleasure that is thus gained, but because they refuse to become involved and to meet the demands that love makes. They are asking for little more than servicing, such as they might get at a gas station. The fact that it may go to bed with a lot of people is less its offense than the fact that it goes to bed with people for whom it does not care.[3]

The decision to have sex should not be governed by what others think. You are, after all, free to choose. The key words, however, are *free but responsible*. This means that not everything you want to do sexually is fine all the time. It doesn't mean, "Do it anytime you feel the urge." It means, rather, "If you do, don't do it just for your own self-interest."

That, of course, is an ideal. As was suggested earlier, we don't always expect or desire a meaningful relationship every time we decide to have sex. It is our nature, as we said, to want pleasure, to satisfy our needs. Everyone is going to experiment, to do things the way they want no matter what anyone says. And that isn't so bad, either. "I don't believe in sex before marriage," one high school junior told me. "But I don't always do what I believe. That's impossible. But I try."

She's right. All you can do is try. It takes a lot of discipline, and sometimes a lot of time. It takes a willingness, sometimes, to listen to an unpopular viewpoint.

Sex can be fun, even if you're not married or not in love. To suggest otherwise would be unfair, for sexual pleasure is one of the most exquisite of human experiences. But there is wide agreement that if you care deeply for each other as partners — and I don't mean in the facetious way one student meant when he said that he has sex only when he falls in love and that's once a week — then your sexual relationship becomes something really special, really better. Two people who are attuned to each other's feelings cannot help getting more enjoyment out of anything they do together, not just sex. You know how it feels to make someone you like happy by giving them a gift they've wanted for a long time. Or how it feels to receive one yourself from a special person. And what about those times you've seen some breathtaking natural beauty and you were alone? You wished that the one who means the most to you were with you so you could share it. And if there wasn't anyone special in your life, you wished there were.

A few years ago, the United Church of Christ distributed a statement on sexual ethics to its seven thousand congregations. Its message was that sex should not be regarded as a furtive and

shameful activity to be hedged about with prohibitions. "Sex
. . . is good as a form of unity and communication between
persons," the church said.

As the most intimate of relations, it is a means of conveying
love for another for whom one has the highest regard. If we
as a church condone sexual union as a communicative act,
can we and should we condone it only within the institution
of marriage? It seems that the only answer we can give is
that sexual union as a communicative act is one of deep
meaning and privacy we can condone only when a man and
a woman are deeply and mutually committed to the fulfill-
ing of each other's personhood.

Implicit in that statement is that sexual intercourse is permis-
sible in or out of marriage, provided the relationship between
the partners is deep and sincere, if the couple is truly in love.

It has been suggested, too, that although more young people
are having sex today, the average number of partners has not
risen. This means that many of those who do have sexual intercourse engage in it only with the ones they truly care for or
plan to marry. If this is true, it means that unmarried young
people are far more loyal to their partners than are husbands
and wives, a great many of whom admit to cheating on their
mates.

Again, it is difficult to live up to ideals. But ideals are real,
not figments of your imagination. They exist, as the American
educator John Dewey said, in character and personality and
action — in short, in people all around us. So, qualities like
loyalty, honesty and responsibility are not just made out of fluff,
although it is easy to think of them that way when they stand
alone as words without bodies. It is trite but true that the best

way to improve our lives, to put as many ideals as possible into practice, is to stay close to the people and things that can show us how. We are in charge, but we all need a compass now and then, something we can rely on for direction. Sometimes we learn from models like church leaders, inspirational literature and decent friends. But we can also learn from those people and things that are not generally considered to be the best models. We can imitate them if we choose, for we do tend to emulate what we admire. That's up to us. But we can also react, that is, move in the opposite direction. Sometimes being exposed to actions that are decidedly wrong makes us think twice before we do them. Or, listening to someone's strong opposing views may make us even more glad that we hold the ones we do. This, of course, can work both ways, and we might stick closer to the wrong values the more we hear about the correct ones. Again, that is up to us. But, more of us do right than wrong — and we do it most of the time. What it amounts to is learning from experience, from others' as well as your own. If the person you're having sex with is only doing it for kicks, and you're not, you'll know that you're just another face in the crowd when it's over. And if you don't know right away, you'll be aware of it when your once intimate partner doesn't answer your letters or return your phone calls, or passes you by in the hall as though nothing important had ever happened. If you were the one who was going for sex only for your own gratification, and your partner saw something more in it, you'll know about that, too. You'll know about it because your partner might be calling you, or writing you, or might bring up the incident in conversation — and you'll probably be embarrassed that it's even mentioned.

This is probably a good place to make another point. We've implied that sex can be moral outside of marriage, but only if it is loyal, responsible, unselfish, honest and truly joyous. But let's face it, some young people just aren't ready for it. They may be old enough in years, but not emotionally. In fact, many health professionals argue that not only sex but steady dating at too young an age can stand in the way of proper sexual and social development.

Which leads us to those who don't have sex. Some may have felt pressured because they are the last holdouts in the group. They may have had sex reluctantly and found it a most unpleasant experience. Or, they have stuck to their values or their religious beliefs. They may lie whenever anyone asks about their sex life, or they may have told the truth and suffered in silence as some of their friends laughed and called them old-fashioned.

It's not easy to be different, and these days, at least in some countries, not having sex *is* being different. But it is important that you continue to be yourself, for it is true, as the German philosopher Arthur Schopenhauer said, "We forfeit three-fourths of ourselves in order to be like other people."

Remember, also, that not everyone who abstains from sex is emotionally deficient, or needs a psychiatrist. Sex, after all, is not the only ingredient in a relationship, and if you depend on it to hold it all together, you're deluding yourself. We've said also that we don't need sex as we need food and drink. Many nuns and priests, as you know, along with other people who don't live in religious communities, live perfectly active and productive and well-adjusted lives without sex. This does not mean that they don't have a sex drive, that they're all repressed individuals. It's simply that they've channeled their energies into other things; they've learned how to assign sex a lower priority. A recent *New York Times* article suggests that this may not be the oddity most people believe it to be. The article quotes a social scientist who was so caught up in a research project that four months went by before he realized, "Hey, I haven't had sex with anybody for a long time." He added: "That seemed okay, and I didn't feel the need for a romantic relationship with a woman until six months later. It wasn't that difficult. What I missed most was not sex, but the closeness you feel in a primary relationship. I learned a lot about myself and about sex."[4]

A few years ago, a Yale University physician made a strong case for people who feel the need to resist pressures to conform sexually. Writing in the *Yale Journal of Biology and Medicine,* Dr. Richard V. Lee recommended that physicians talk about the medical value of virginity and chastity in their advice to young people. "We boast to our young people about our great breakthroughs in preventing pregnancy and treating venereal disease, disregarding the most reliable and specific, the least expensive and toxic, preventative of both gestational and venereal distress, the ancient, honorable and even healthy state of virginity," he said. Freedom from the fear of pregnancy and sexual inadequacy are surely desirable, Dr. Lee wrote, but in no way imply freedom to indulge in sexual license. "Yet, this is an equation that some physicians inadvertently present to a hormonally chaotic, impulsive and sensually aroused adolescent market."[5]

Dr. Lee, who is a professor of internal medicine and a venereal-disease specialist, added that he was not anxious to slow down productive research into human sexuality, or to urge a stringent moralistic approach in the doctor's management of sexual problems. "It does seem to me, however," he said, "that chastity is an important aspect of medical management deserving as much careful thought and research as orgasm. Nor do I wish to re-establish a puritanical new Victorian cult of the virgin. However, these young people who do aspire to remain chaste need as much reassurance that their choice is healthy and of value as those who choose sexual liberation. . . . In this age of apparent moral chaos and sexual liberation, the virgin and open advocacy of virginity for young people seem to have become undesirable anachronisms."[6]

We all have to exercise some degree of control over our sexuality, and that's not an easy job in many cases. For those who choose a life of abstinence, or even temporary abstinence, the job becomes even more difficult. But there is little doubt that self-control is one of humankind's highest qualities. If you can develop it, if you can learn to be the master and mistress of your passions, then it's certain that you'll learn how to control other circumstances in your life. Self-discipline gets things done, whether it is dealing with a life crisis or painting a picture. Waiting before you have sex, either waiting for marriage or for the right person to come along, develops your self-control. And you'll probably need it many times in life. Holding off might also strengthen the bond between you and your partner, and if you marry, the vow that you take to be loyal and loving may mean more because you've already learned how to promise yourselves to each other.

Granted, all of this is easier said than done, and is not for everyone. Promises, whether made to parents or to the person we decide to live with, may be fun to make. But they are difficult to keep. Nonetheless, they are a reflection of our sincerity, and it may sometimes be nicer to have a promise broken than none made.

A decision not to have sex is as serious a one as a decision to go ahead. Deciding against it often means you'll have to do some private agonizing, either because you have to keep strong emotions and desires in check, or because your friends regard you as some kind of freak. It means that you may have to be brutally frank with people who bug you about it, or who try to get you to go along. You might just have to say, "Look, I don't and that's it." You also may be fortunate enough to have a good many friends who feel as you do. Having at least a few people around who think as you do on moral issues is a way of taking the pressure off.

Sex is not a matter to take lightly when you engage in it, but sometimes, injecting a little humor into a situation makes it more bearable, and takes the heat off. If you're a young woman, maybe this quote from an 1892 book of etiquette will baffle the sex jock who's after you: "The association of men and women in refined circles shall be frank without freedom, friendly without familiarity. Every well-bred woman is a queen for whose sake every well-bred man will hold a lance in rest."

Or you might try the advice of a Chicago physician mentioned earlier, Dr. Lonny Myers, who suggested this method of teaching young women how to minimize unwanted seductions: "It's easy. Just take the mystery out of the typical line. Make a list of them, you know them all. 'I love you more than anything.' 'I'll kill myself if you don't go to bed with me.' 'It's not healthy to pet without intercourse.' Then talk about them, sing them in a chorus, put them up on the wall and joke about them. That should do it."[7]

This approach might be more difficult for a young man to follow because the male has traditionally been the pursuer, and the woman the pursued in a sex relationship. But while more young women are, in fact, openly aggressive sexually today, and some young men feel pressured to perform, a young man generally feels he must have sex to satisfy his ego, to enable him

to live up to "expectations." He might believe he is being compared to other young men his partner might have had. Because
of the male's conventional role, avoidance of sex for him is often
a most difficult and trying experience. On the one hand he wants
to prove himself, but on the other he may have values that say
that you don't have sex unless you're in love or planning to
marry. It presents the classic moral dilemma — the situation
in which there is a conflict of duties. The only way out of it is
for him to be honest and determine which course of action takes
precedence *for him*. It takes common sense, that instinctive sense
that allows us to size up a problem and make a decision. It may
not mean too much in a philosopher's handbook, but make no
mistake: there is wisdom in it, and a handful of sense, as a
Spanish proverb has it, is worth a bushel of learning.

It may take time to make the right decisions about sex, and
you may make promises that you cannot keep. But that's life,
and sex is a vital part of it. Sex will never lose its mystery or
its appeal, and we can be thankful for that. We'll never lose
our hang-ups about it either, no matter how many books are
written or how blurred the sex roles become. Because it is a
unique experience, it will continue to affect us all in strange
ways. All we can do is accept it as another fact of life, and treat
it with the respect it deserves.

Epilogue

THERE WAS, in ancient Greece, a philosopher named Aristippus. He lived in Cyrene and was a disciple of Socrates. Aristippus founded the Cyrenaic School of Hedonists, which was dedicated to the proposition that pleasure is life's goal, and that care should be taken to avoid pain.

Once, he said of his mistress: "She doesn't love me? Why should I care? I don't think that wine or fish have any love for me, and yet I consume them with pleasure."

Cyrenaics believed, as should be obvious from Aristippus's comment, that everyone should gratify his or her own desires without regard for the feelings of others. They put all of their energy into living for the moment, not for the future.

Not all hedonists took so strong a stand, however. There were the Epicureans, a school founded by the philosopher Epicurus that also taught that pleasure was the highest good. Their motto, in fact, was *Dum vivimus vivamus* (While we live, let us enjoy

life). But these hedonists, also known as rational hedonists, believed that one should seek out long-lasting pleasures instead of
the intense, fleeting ones pursued by the Cyrenaics. For Epicurus,
such enduring pleasures could be attained only through reason
and were mental rather than physical ones — music apprecia-
tion, reading, a peaceful state of mind. Unfortunately, many
people thought (and still do) that Epicureans espoused a life of
eating, drinking and merrymaking. On the contrary, their idea
of "good living" meant "good" in the highest sense, and they
stressed self-control and prudence in daily life.

Said Epicurus:

When we say that pleasure is the aim and end, we do not
mean the pleasures of the prodigal or the pleasures of sen-
suality, as we are understood by some to do through igno-
rance, prejudice or wilful misrepresentation. By pleasure
we mean the absence of pain in the body and of trouble in
the soul. It is not an unbroken succession of drinking bouts
and revelry, not sexual love, not the enjoyment of fish and
other delicacies of a luxurious table which produce a pleasant life; it is sober reasoning, searching out the grounds of
every choice and avoidance, and banishing those beliefs
through which the greatest tumults take possession of the
soul.[1]

Hedonists of both schools, Epicurean and Cyrenaic, are still
with us, and you probably could fit many of your friends and
relatives into one or the other category, or into a blend of each.
You yourself have a certain view of pleasure and of having fun,
and quite possibly it's the most important thing in your life
right now. It would also be silly to suggest that pleasure and
your own happiness are things to be shunned, and that an

altruistic way of life — that is, one of benevolent interest in the well-being of others — is a road we should follow all of the time. We will always be torn between our own desires and those of others, between looking out for ourselves and for our fellow citizens. But we do have to think of ourselves, too.

We have to be prepared, however, to think about the feelings of others *every so often;* we ought to be ready to sacrifice our own interests once in a while. We must be ready to forgo certain pleasures if they must be obtained by injuring another or by making him or her unhappy.

The good thing is that it's never too late to learn, and we do have the power to override many of the unfavorable early influences in our lives that could stand in the way. If we refuse to use that ability to learn from people and situations, then so much the worse for us. We'll end up blaming others for our faults.

Showing true affection is more than sending someone a card postmarked Loveland, Colorado, or Valentines, Nebraska. It's learning how to put some of what has been talked about here into practice. When you can do that, you'll have earned the right to say, "I love you."

Notes

Introduction

1. Kenneth B. Murphy, "Hub Priest Sees Good in Youths' Love-Ins," *Boston Traveler*, April 27, 1967.

1. Friendship / Liking / Loving

1. Theodore Reik, *Of Love and Lust* (New York: Farrar, Straus, 1949), pp. 19, 20, 22.
2. Philip G. Zimbardo, *Psychology and Life* (Glenview, Ill.: Scott, Foresman, 1975), p. 5.
3. H. Rackham, *Preface to Philosophy: Book of Readings* (New York: Macmillan, 1950), p. 91.
4. Zimbardo, p. 578.
5. Robert Brain, *Friends and Lovers* (New York: Basic Books, 1976), p. 265.

2. Knowing, and Liking, Yourself

1. Lecomte de Noüy, *Human Destiny* (New York: McKay, 1947), p. xix.
2. Dale Carnegie, *How to Win Friends and Influence People* (New York: Simon and Schuster, 1936), p. 103.
3. Leo Buscaglia, *Love* (New York: Fawcett Books, 1972), p. 138.
4. George Weinberg, *Self Creation* (New York: St. Martin's Press, 1978), p. 148.
5. Elaine Walster, *A New Look at Love* (Reading, Mass.: Addison-Wesley, 1978), pp. 110–111.

3. Homosexuality

1. Charles W. Socarides in *Journal of the American Medical Association*, May 18, 1970.
2. Bernard Riess in *The Sciences*, Oct. 1972.
3. W. H. Masters and V. E. Johnson, *Homosexuality in Perspective* (Boston: Little, Brown, 1979), p. 411.
4. Samuel DeMilia in the *New York Times*, Feb. 10, 1978.
5. "Gays on the March," *Time* magazine, Sept. 9, 1975.
6. *New York Times*, Feb. 10, 1978.

4. Jealousy

1. George and Nena O'Neill, *Open Marriage* (New York: M. Evans, 1972), pp. 239–40.
2. Gordon Clanton and Lynn Smith in *Psychology Today*, March 1977.
3. Ibid.
4. Ibid.
5. Dorothy Barash, "Marital Therapy," *Menninger Perspective*, Spring 1978.

5. Pornography

1. Will Durant, *Caesar and Christ* (New York: Simon and Schuster, 1944), p. 458.
2. Herant A. Katchadourian and Donald T. Lunde, *Fundamentals of Human Sexuality* (New York: Holt, Rinehart and Winston, 1972), pp. 322–23.
3. *Chicago Sun-Times*, Mar. 27, 1966.
4. Malcolm Boyd in the *New York Times*, Aug. 5, 1973.
5. Ibid.
6. J. W. Money in *Medical World News*, Mar. 12, 1971.
7. Ezekiel Green, "Taking Back the Night," in the *San Francisco Sunday Examiner and Chronicle*'s *California Living*, Feb. 11, 1979.

6. Prostitution

1. Herodotus, quoted in Will Durant, *Our Oriental Heritage* (New York: Simon and Schuster, 1954), p. 245.

2. Alfred Kinsey, *Sexual Behavior in the Human Female* (Philadelphia: W. B. Saunders, 1953), p. 323.

3. "The Shooting of Judy," *Boston Herald American,* Sept. 28, 1978.

4. Studs Terkel, *Working* (New York: Pantheon Books, 1972), p. 59.

5. Susan Brownmiller, *Against Our Will* (New York: Simon and Schuster, 1975), p. 391.

7. Marriage / Living Together

1. Margaret Reedy, paper presented at the American Psychological Association meetings, Toronto, Sept. 1978.

2. John Langone, *Vital Signs* (Boston: Little, Brown, 1974), p. 289.

3. Dorothy Barash, "Marital Therapy," in *Menninger Perspective,* Spring 1978.

4. Ibid.

8. Sex Education

1. *American Medical News,* Oct. 27, 1978.

2. *Family Planning Perspectives,* July/August 1978.

3. Lonny Myers, quoted in Joann Rodgers, "She'd Teach Second Graders about Sex," *Boston Herald American,* Nov. 11, 1977.

9. Sex and Morality

1. Havelock Ellis, *The Psychology of Sex* (Philadelphia: F. A. Davis, 1901), p. 16.

2. Albert Ellis, address at Michigan State University, Feb. 18, 1969.

3. Henry Fairlie, *The Seven Deadly Sins Today,* quoted in the *Boston Globe,* Oct. 16, 1977.

4. Georgia Dullea, "A Lack of Sexual Desire Emerges As a Contemporary Condition," *New York Times,* May 1, 1978.

5. Richard V. Lee, *Yale Journal of Biology and Medicine,* vol. 45, no. 5 (1972).

6. Ibid.

7. Lonny Myers, quoted in Joann Rodgers, "She'd Teach Second Graders about Sex," *Boston Herald American,* Nov. 11, 1977.

Epilogue

1. Epicurus, from *Letter to Menoeceus,* in the tenth book of Diogenes Laertius, translated by C. D. Yonge (London: G. Bell and Sons, 1909).

Index